4B

Math in Focus®

Singapore Math
by Marshall Cavendish

Extra Practice

Author
Bernice Lau Pui Wah

Marshall Cavendish
Education

US Distributor

HOUGHTON MIFFLIN HARCOURT

COMMON CORE

© Copyright 2009, 2013 Edition Marshall Cavendish International (Singapore) Private Limited

Published by Marshall Cavendish Education
An imprint of Marshall Cavendish International (Singapore) Private Limited
Times Centre, 1 New Industrial Road, Singapore 536196
Customer Service Hotline: (65) 6411 0820
E-mail: tmesales@sg.marshallcavendish.com
Website: www.marshallcavendish.com/education

Distributed by
Houghton Mifflin Harcourt
222 Berkeley Street
Boston, MA 02116
Tel: 617-351-5000
Website: www.hmheducation.com/mathinfocus

First published 2009
2013 Edition

Math in Focus® Extra Practice 4B
ISBN 978-0-669-01572-0

Printed in Singapore

4 5 6 7 8   1401   18 17 16 15 14 13
4500404079   A B C D E

Contents

CHAPTER 7 Decimals

Lesson 7.1 Understanding Tenths	1
Lesson 7.2 Understanding Hundredths	7
Lesson 7.3 Comparing Decimals (Part 1)	13
Lesson 7.3 Comparing Decimals (Part 2)	15
Lesson 7.4 Rounding Decimals (Part 1)	17
Lesson 7.4 Rounding Decimals (Part 2)	19
Lesson 7.5 Fractions and Decimals	21

Put on Your Thinking Cap!   **23**

CHAPTER 8 Adding and Subtracting Decimals

Lesson 8.1 Adding Decimals (Part 1)	25
Lesson 8.1 Adding Decimals (Part 2)	27
Lesson 8.2 Subtracting Decimals	29
Lesson 8.3 Real-World Problems: Decimals	31

Put on Your Thinking Cap!   **35**

CHAPTER 9 Angles

Lesson 9.1 Understanding and Measuring Angles	37
Lesson 9.2 Drawing Angles to 180°	43
Lesson 9.3 Turns and Right Angles	45

Put on Your Thinking Cap!   **47**

CHAPTER 10

Perpendicular and Parallel Line Segments

Lesson 10.1 Drawing Perpendicular Line Segments	49
Lesson 10.2 Drawing Parallel Line Segments	51
Lesson 10.3 Horizontal and Vertical Lines	53
Put on Your Thinking Cap!	**55**

CHAPTER 11

Squares and Rectangles

Lesson 11.1 Squares and Rectangles	59
Lesson 11.2 Properties of Squares and Rectangles	65
Put on Your Thinking Cap!	67

Test Prep for Chapters 7 to 11	**69**

CHAPTER 12

Area and Perimeter

Lesson 12.1 Area of a Rectangle	77
Lesson 12.2 Rectangles and Squares (Part 1)	83
Lesson 12.2 Rectangles and Squares (Part 2)	85
Lesson 12.3 Composite Figures	89
Lesson 12.4 Using Formulas for Area and Perimeter	93
Put on Your Thinking Cap!	**97**

CHAPTER 13 Symmetry

Lesson 13.1   Identifying Lines of Symmetry   99
Lesson 13.2   Rotational Symmetry   101
Lesson 13.3   Making Symmetric Shapes and Patterns   103

Put on Your Thinking Cap!   **105**

CHAPTER 14 Tessellations

Lesson 14.1   Identifying Tessellations   107
Lesson 14.2   More Tessellations   117

Put on Your Thinking Cap!   **123**

End-of-Year Test   **125**
Answers   **139**

Introducing

Math in Focus®

Extra Practice

Extra Practice 4A and 4B, written to complement *Math in Focus®: Singapore Math by Marshall Cavendish* Grade 4, offer further practice very similar to the Practice exercises in the Student Books and Workbooks for on-level students.

Extra Practice provides ample questions to reinforce all the concepts taught, and includes challenging questions in the Put on Your Thinking Cap! pages. These pages provide extra non-routine problem-solving opportunities, strengthening critical thinking skills.

Extra Practice is an excellent option for homework, or may be used in class or after school. It is intended for students who simply need more practice to become confident, or secure students who are aiming for excellence.

Name: _____ **Date:** _____

CHAPTER 7 Decimals

Lesson 7.1   Understanding Tenths

Write the decimals that the shaded and unshaded parts represent.

1.

shaded parts: _____

unshaded parts: _____

2.

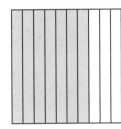

shaded parts: _____

unshaded parts: _____

3.

shaded parts: _____

unshaded parts: _____

4.

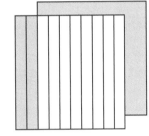

shaded parts: _____

unshaded parts: _____

5.

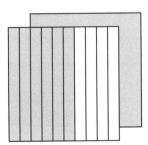

shaded parts: _____

unshaded parts: _____

6.

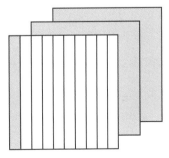

shaded parts: _____

unshaded parts: _____

Write a decimal for each place-value chart.

7.

Ones	Tenths
	○ ○ ○ ○ ○
	○ ○ ○ ○

_____

8.

Ones	Tenths
○ ○ ○	○ ○

_____

Write the correct decimal in each box.

9.

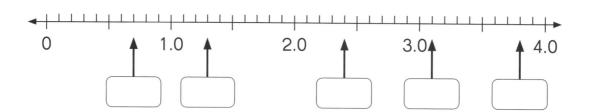

10.

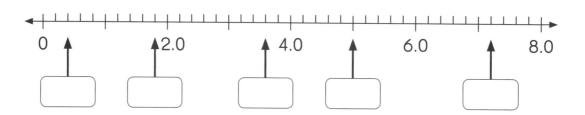

● **Write each of these as a decimal.**

11. 4 tenths = _____   12. 25 tenths = _____

13. 68 tenths = _____   14. 176 tenths = _____

15. 3 ones and 9 tenths = _____

16. 40 ones and 2 tenths = _____

Write each fraction or mixed number as a decimal.

17. $\frac{6}{10}$ = _____   18. $\frac{9}{10}$ = _____

19. $4\frac{8}{10}$ = _____   20. $7\frac{2}{10}$ = _____

● 21. $16\frac{1}{10}$ = _____   22. $44\frac{5}{10}$ = _____

23. $\frac{63}{10}$ = _____   24. $\frac{50}{10}$ = _____

25. $\frac{210}{10}$ = _____   26. $\frac{201}{10}$ = _____

27. $\frac{300}{10}$ = _____   28. $\frac{330}{10}$ = _____

Write each number as a fraction and as a decimal.
Complete the table.

	Number of Tenths	Fraction	Decimal
29.	6 tenths		
30.	19 tenths		
31.	57 tenths		
32.	124 tenths		
33.	203 tenths		
34.	455 tenths		

Write a fraction and a decimal for each measure.

35. Length of paper clip = [ ] cm

= [ ] cm

36. Weight of pumpkin = [ ] lb

= [ ] lb

Write a fraction and a decimal for the measure.

37.   Volume of water = ☐ L

= ☐ L

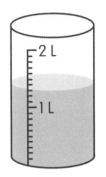

Fill in the blanks.

38.   8.9 = 8 ones and _____ tenths

39.   16.4 = 1 ten _____ ones and 4 tenths

40.   37.2 = 3 tens 7 ones and _____ tenths

41.   58.6 = _____ tens 8 ones and 6 tenths

42.   90.5 = _____ tens _____ ones and 5 tenths

15.2 can be written as $10 + 5 + \dfrac{2}{10}$. Complete in the same way.

43.   5.2 = ☐ + ☐

44.   16.3 = ☐ + ☐ + ☐

14.3 can be written as $10 + 4 + 0.3$. Complete in the same way.

45.   8.4 = ☐ + ☐

46.   70.9 = ☐ + ☐ + ☐

Fill in the blanks.

47.

Tens	Ones	Tenths
2	4	7

The digit 7 is in the _____ place. Its value is _____.

48.

Tens	Ones	Tenths
3	8	5

The digit 8 is in the _____ place. Its value is _____.

49.

Tens	Ones	Tenths
6	0	9

The digit _____ is in the tens place. Its value is _____.

50.

Tens	Ones	Tenths
8	1	4

The digit _____ is in the tenths place. Its value is _____.

Lesson 7.2   Understanding Hundredths

Write the decimals that the shaded and unshaded parts represent.

1.

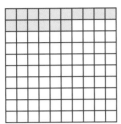

shaded parts: _____

unshaded parts: _____

2.

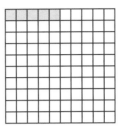

shaded parts: _____

unshaded parts: _____

3.

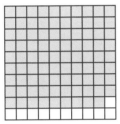

shaded parts: _____

unshaded parts: _____

4.

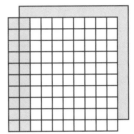

shaded parts: _____

unshaded parts: _____

5.

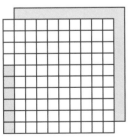

shaded parts: _____

unshaded parts: _____

6.

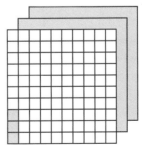

shaded parts: _____

unshaded parts: _____

Write a decimal for each place-value chart.

7.

Ones	Tenths	Hundredths
	○ ○ ○ ○ ○	○ ○ ○

_____

8.

Ones	Tenths	Hundredths
○ ○ ○		○ ○ ○ ○ ○ ○ ○ ○

_____

Write the correct decimal in each box.

9.

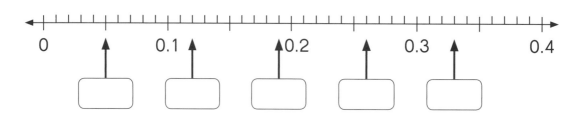

10.

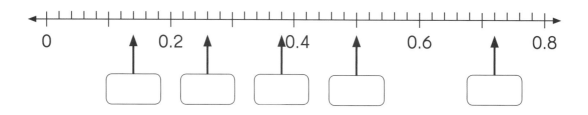

Write each of these as a decimal.

11.   9 hundredths = _____   **12.**   10 hundredths = _____

13.   35 hundredths = _____   **14.**   206 hundredths = _____

15.   8 tenths 6 hundredths = _____

16.   41 ones and 3 hundredths = _____

17.   50 ones and 22 hundredths = _____

Write each fraction or mixed number as a decimal.

18. $\dfrac{4}{100}$ = _____   **19.** $\dfrac{19}{100}$ = _____

20. $\dfrac{65}{100}$ = _____   **21.** $\dfrac{80}{100}$ = _____

22. $2\dfrac{14}{100}$ = _____   **23.** $15\dfrac{3}{100}$ = _____

24. $30\dfrac{8}{100}$ = _____   **25.** $\dfrac{169}{100}$ = _____

26. $\dfrac{202}{100}$ = _____   **27.** $\dfrac{250}{100}$ = _____

Write each decimal in hundredths.

28.   0.08 = _____ hundredths   **29.**   0.25 = _____ hundredths

30.   0.40 = _____ hundredths   **31.**   6.07 = _____ hundredths

32.   5.39 = _____ hundredths   **33.**   9.80 = _____ hundredths

**Write each number as a fraction and as a decimal.
Complete the table.**

	Number of Hundredths	Fraction	Decimal
34.	1 hundredth		
35.	6 hundredths		
36.	9 hundredths		
37.	13 hundredths		
38.	59 hundredths		
39.	106 hundredths		

Fill in the blanks.

40. $0.75 =$ _____ tenths _____ hundredths

41. $3.46 = 3$ _____ and 4 tenths _____ hundredths

42. $5.08 = 5$ ones and _____ hundredths

43. $6.23 =$ _____ ones and _____ tenths _____ hundredths

44. $9.50 =$ _____ ones and _____ tenths _____ hundredths

6.13 can be written as $6 + \frac{1}{10} + \frac{3}{100}$. Complete in the same way.

45. $1.56 = \boxed{} + \boxed{} + \boxed{}$

46. $24.07 = \boxed{} + \boxed{} + \boxed{} + \boxed{}$

7.45 can be written as $7 + 0.4 + 0.05$. Complete in the same way.

47. $3.89 = \boxed{} + \boxed{} + \boxed{}$

48. $51.52 = \boxed{} + \boxed{} + \boxed{} + \boxed{}$

Fill in the blanks.

49.

Ones	Tenths	Hundredths
4	8	3

The digit 3 is in the _____ place. Its value is _____.

50.

Ones	Tenths	Hundredths
7	0	9

The digit 0 is in the _____ place. Its value is _____.

51.

Tens	Ones		Tenths	Hundredths
6	1	•	5	5

The digit _____ is in the tens place. Its value is _____.

52.

Tens	Ones		Tenths	Hundredths
3	4	•	0	2

The digit _____ is in the hundredths place. Its value is _____.

Write each amount in decimal form.

53.   35 cents = $_____

54.   70 cents = $_____

55.   108 cents = $_____

56.   240 cents = $_____

57.   6 dollars 35 cents = $_____

58.   9 dollars 5 cents = $_____

Lesson 7.3   Comparing Decimals (Part 1)

Use the number line. Find the number that is

1.0   1.1   1.2   1.3   1.4   1.5   1.6   1.7   1.8   1.9   2.0

1.   0.1 more than 1.9.   _____

2.   0.3 more than 1.1.   _____

3.   0.5 more than 1.4.   _____

4.   0.4 less than 1.6.   _____

5.   0.2 less than 1.8.   _____

Use the number line. Find the number that is

1.20   1.21   1.22   1.23   1.24   1.25   1.26   1.27   1.28   1.29   1.30

6.   0.01 more than 1.26.   _____

7.   0.02 more than 1.23.   _____

8.   0.05 more than 1.24.   _____

9.   0.03 less than 1.26.   _____

10.   0.04 less than 1.25.   _____

Continue the number patterns.
Use the number line to help you.

11.

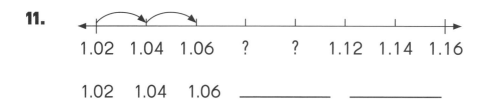

1.02 1.04 1.06   ?   ?   1.12 1.14 1.16

1.02   1.04   1.06   _____   _____

12.

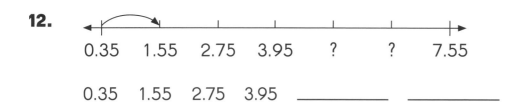

0.35   1.55   2.75   3.95   ?   ?   7.55

0.35   1.55   2.75   3.95   _____   _____

13.

5.92   5.60   5.28   ?   ?   4.32   4.00

5.92   5.60   5.28   _____   _____

14.

7.95   6.75   5.55   ?   ?   1.95   0.75

7.95   6.75   5.55   _____   _____

15.

6.34   6.38   6.28   ?   6.22   ?   6.16

6.34   6.38   6.28   _____   6.22   _____   6.16

Lesson 7.3   Comparing Decimals (Part 2)

Compare the two decimals in each table. Then fill in the blanks.

1.

Ones		Tenths	Hundredths
2	.	0	3
2	.	0	6

_____ is greater than _____.

2.

Ones		Tenths	Hundredths
0	.	3	5
0	.	3	2

_____ is less than _____.

3.

Ones		Tenths	Hundredths
8	.	2	3
8	.	3	2

_____ is greater than _____.

4.

Ones		Tenths	Hundredths
0	.	0	9
0	.	9	0

_____ is less than _____.

Compare. Write < or >.

5.   0.58 ( ) 0.85

6.   0.07 ( ) 0.09

7.   3.36 ( ) 3.63

8.   2.10 ( ) 2.01

Circle the greatest decimal and underline the least.

9.   0.45   0.15   0.54

10.   7.68   7.86   6.78

Write the decimals in order from least to greatest.

11.   0.86 0.82 0.68 _____ _____ _____

12.   0.98 0.99 0.89 _____ _____ _____

13.   0.75 0.57 0.70 _____ _____ _____

14.   5.46 6.54 5.64 _____ _____ _____

Write the decimals in order from greatest to least.

15.   0.10 0.09 0.07 _____ _____ _____

16.   0.99 0.09 0.90 _____ _____ _____

17.   0.38 0.83 3.08 _____ _____ _____

18.   8.49 9.48 8.94 _____ _____ _____

Lesson 7.4   Rounding Decimals (Part 1)

Fill in the missing number in each box.
Then round each decimal to the nearest whole number.

1.

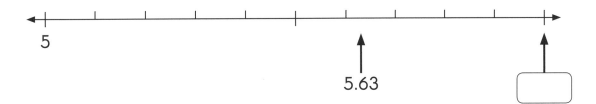

5.63 rounded to the nearest whole number is _____.

2.

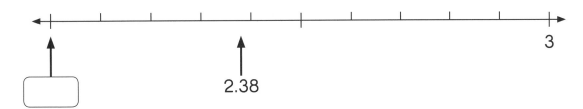

2.38 rounded to the nearest whole number is _____.

Round each measure.

3.

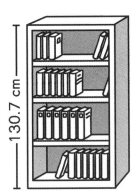

Round the height of the cabinet to the nearest centimeter.

_____ centimeters is about _____ centimeters.

4.

Round the amount of water to the nearest liter.

_____ liters is about _____ liters.

5.

Round the weight of the grapes to the nearest pound.

_____ pounds is about _____ pounds.

6.

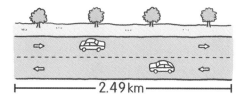

Round the length of the road to the nearest kilometer.

_____ kilometers is about _____ kilometers.

7.

Round the price of the sneakers to the nearest dollar.

$_____ is about _____ dollars.

Lesson 7.4   Rounding Decimals (Part 2)

Fill in the missing number in each box. Then round each decimal to the nearest tenth.

1.

3.0   3.08

3.08 rounded to the nearest tenth is _____.

2.

13.2

13.13

13.13 rounded to the nearest tenth is _____.

Round each measure.

3.   The weight of a kitten is 2.05 pounds.
Round the weight of the kitten to the nearest tenth of a pound.

2.05 pounds is about _____ pounds.

4.   The length of a bed is 1.34 meters.
Round the length of the bed to the nearest tenth of a meter.

_____ meters is about _____ meters.

5.   Cedar Highway is 15.59 kilometers long.
Round the length of the highway to the nearest tenth of a kilometer.

_____ kilometers is about _____ kilometers.

6. The volume of water in a jug is 3.46 liters.
Round the volume of water to the nearest liter.

_____ liters is about _____ liters.

7. Jason's weight is 96.52 pounds.
Round Jason's weight to the nearest pound.

_____ pounds is about _____ pounds.

Round each decimal to the nearest whole number and then to the nearest tenth.

| | Decimal | Rounded to the nearest | |
		Whole Number	Tenth
8.	0.67		
9.	1.28		
10.	3.06		
11.	8.73		
12.	19.45		
13.	23.99		
14.	36.24		
15.	41.99		

© Marshall Cavendish International (Singapore) Private Limited.

Lesson 7.5   Fractions and Decimals

Write each fraction or mixed number as a decimal.

1.

$$\frac{4}{10} = \text{_____}$$

2.
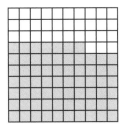

$$\frac{67}{100} = \text{_____}$$

3. $\frac{3}{10} = \text{_____}$

4. $\frac{49}{100} = \text{_____}$

5. $5\frac{9}{10} = \text{_____}$

6. $8\frac{79}{100} = \text{_____}$

Write each fraction or mixed number as a decimal.
Hint: Make the denominator 10 or 100.

7. $\frac{1}{5} = \dfrac{\boxed{}}{10} = \text{_____}$

8. $\frac{19}{50} = \dfrac{\boxed{}}{100} = \text{_____}$

9. $\frac{4}{5} = \text{_____}$

10. $\frac{1}{2} = \text{_____}$

Write each fraction or mixed number as a decimal.
Hint: Make the denominator 10 or 100.

11. $\dfrac{7}{4} = $ _____

12. $\dfrac{6}{20} = $ _____

13. $\dfrac{16}{25} = $ _____

14. $7\dfrac{1}{5} = $ _____

Write each decimal as a fraction or mixed number in simplest form.

15. $0.6 = $ _____

16. $5.7 = $ _____

17. $1.45 = $ _____

18. $3.36 = $ _____

Put on Your Thinking Cap!

Mark an X to show where each decimal is located on the number line.

1.   3.0

0   0.5   1.0   1.5

2.   0.24

0   0.06   0.12

Write any number that is

3.   greater than 5.3 but less than 5.4.   _____

4.   greater than 0.4 but less than 0.5.   _____

5.   greater than 3.85 but less than 3.95.   _____

Answer the questions.

6.   How many tenths are in 8.32? _____ tenths

7.   How many tenths are in 25.80? _____ tenths

8.   How many tenths are in 37.00? _____ tenths

9.   How many hundredths are in 0.56? _____ hundredths

Answer the questions.

10. How many hundredths are in 1.82? _____ hundredths

11. How many hundredths are in 3.94? _____ hundredths

12. Round 8.99 to the nearest

    a. whole number. _____

    b. tenth. _____

Continue the number patterns.

13.   1.98   4.18   6.38   8.58   10.78   _____

14.   1.8   1.76   1.72   1.68   1.64   _____

15.   1.2   1.7   2.7   4.2   6.2   _____

16.   3.7   3.5   3.1   2.5   1.7   _____

17.   1.68   1.69   1.70   1.68   1.66   1.67   _____

18.   4.92   4.62   4.02   3.12   1.92   _____

19.   6.38   5.98   7.38   6.58   9.38   8.18   _____

CHAPTER 8 Adding and Subtracting Decimals

Lesson 8.1   Adding Decimals (Part 1)

Add.

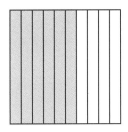 +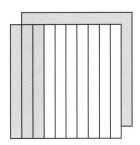

Ones	Tenths
	○ ○ ○ ○ ○ ○
○	○ ○ ○

1.   0.6 + 1.3 = _____

Fill in the blanks. Write each sum as a decimal.

2.   0.5 + 0.7 = _____ tenths + _____ tenths

= _____ tenths

= _____

Fill in the blanks. Write each sum as a decimal.

3.   1.4 + 2.3 = _____ tenths + _____ tenths

= _____ tenths

= _____

Add.

4.   4 . 3
      +   6 . 5
      _____

5.   7 . 8
      + 2 5 . 1
      _____

6.   6 . 9
      + 3 8 . 5
      _____

7.   1 8 . 5
      +   4 . 7
      _____

Write in vertical form. Then add.

8.   8.6 + 26.8 = _____

9.   15.4 + 17.6 = _____

10. 17.9 + 12.6 = _____

11. 20.1 + 19.9 = _____

Lesson 8.1   Adding Decimals (Part 2)

Add.

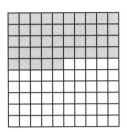 +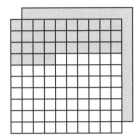

Ones	Tenths	Hundredths
	◯ ◯ ◯ ◯	◯ ◯ ◯ ◯ ◯
◯	◯ ◯ ◯	◯ ◯ ◯ ◯

1.   0.45 + 1.34 = _____

Fill in the blanks. Write each sum as a decimal.

2.   0.71 + 0.29 = _____ hundredths + _____ hundredths

= _____ hundredths

= _____

3.   0.38 + 0.15 = _____ hundredths + _____ hundredths

= _____ hundredths

= _____

Fill in the blanks. Write each sum as a decimal.

4. 0.65 + 0.45 = _____ hundredths + _____ hundredths

= _____ hundredths

= _____

Add.

5.
$$
\begin{array}{r}
\$5.94 \\
+\$25.05 \\
\hline
\end{array}
$$

6.
$$
\begin{array}{r}
\$4.63 \\
+\$17.54 \\
\hline
\end{array}
$$

7.
$$
\begin{array}{r}
\$17.55 \\
+\$26.79 \\
\hline
\end{array}
$$

8.
$$
\begin{array}{r}
\$38.69 \\
+\$18.58 \\
\hline
\end{array}
$$

Write in vertical form. Then add.

9. $0.08 + $0.51 = $_____   **10.** $0.37 + $0.85 = $_____

11. $0.79 + $0.57 = $_____   **12.** $0.65 + $0.78 = $_____

Lesson 8.2   Subtracting Decimals

Subtract.

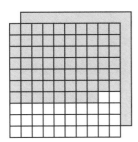 –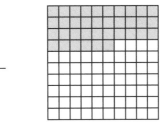

Ones	Tenths	Hundredths
◯	◯ ◯ ◯ ◯ ◯ ◯	◯ ◯ ◯ ◯ ◯ ◯ ◯ ◯ ◯
	◯ ◯ ◯	◯ ◯ ◯ ◯ ◯ ◯

1. $1.68 - 0.36 = $ _____

Fill in the blanks. Write the difference as a decimal.

2. $2.5 - 0.8 = $ _____ tenths $-$ _____ tenths

= _____ tenths

= _____

3. $3.4 - 0.9 = $ _____ tenths $-$ _____ tenths

= _____ tenths

= _____

4.   0.32 − 0.17 = _____ hundredths − _____ hundredths

= _____ hundredths

= _____

5.   0.21 − 0.07 = _____ hundredths − _____ hundredths

= _____ hundredths

= _____

Subtract.

6.   0 . 9 0
         − 0 . 2 7
         _____

7.   0 . 8 1
         − 0 . 3 6
         _____

8.   0 . 7 4
         − 0 . 4 5
         _____

9.   6 . 9
         − 6 . 2
         _____

10.   7 . 0
          − 3 . 1
          _____

11.   1 2 . 3
          −   7 . 4
          _____

Write in vertical form. Then subtract.

12.   16.57 − 8.23 = _____

13.   21.04 − 6.52 = _____

14.   30.06 − 18.97 = _____

15.   44.99 − 26.23 = _____

Lesson 8.3   Real-World Problems: Decimals

Solve. Show your work.

1. The weight of a bag of potatoes is 2.5 pounds. Ms. Bennett uses 0.55 pound of potatoes on the first day and 1.08 pounds on the second day. How many pounds of potatoes are left?

2. Ms. Petrie buys some peaches for $4.95 and some breakfast cereal for $7.85. Ms. Petrie had $50 before she went shopping. How much money does Ms. Petrie have left after she buys the peaches and cereal?

3. The total weight of Container A and Container B is 71.4 pounds. The total weight of Container B and Container C is 58.5 pounds. The weight of Container C is 29.7 pounds. What is the weight of Container A?

4. In a long jump competition, Paul jumps 0.16 meter farther than Royston. Shawn jumps 0.24 meter less than Paul. Shawn jumps a distance of 1.04 meters. How far does Royston jump?

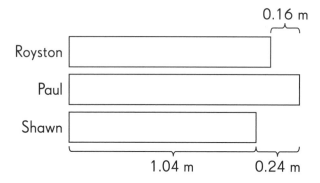

5. The distance between John's home and his school is 7.49 kilometers.
The distance from John's school to the Tennis Academy is 9.87 kilometers.

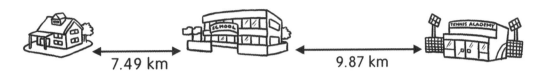

7.49 km   9.87 km

a. John travels from home to school and then to the Academy.
How far does John travel?

b. After his tennis class, John goes back to school. What is the total
distance John travels?

6. Greg makes a kite using the following materials.

KITE MATERIALS	
1 long stick	60 cm
1 short stick	45.8 cm
1 tail	3.6 m
1 ball of string	180 m

a. How much shorter is the short stick than the long stick?

b. How many long sticks put end to end will be needed to equal the total length of the tail?

Name: _____ Date: _____

Put on Your Thinking Cap!

Solve. Show your work.

1. Find the result when you subtract the sum of 3.68 and 8.97 from 20.02.

2. Bernard has $6.00 less than Andy but $2.75 more than Calvin. How much more money does Andy have than Calvin?

Use the given information to answer the questions.

School Sale		
Item	**Regular Price**	**Sale Price**
Ballpoint Pen	$2.30	$1.95
Correction Pen	$3.50	$2.75
Mechanical Pencil	$1.20	$0.85

3. How much do you save when you buy 3 ballpoint pens on sale instead of at the regular price?

4. Julio buys 2 mechanical pencils and a correction pen at the sale price. He gives the cashier a $10 bill. How much change does Julio get back?

5. Nicolas bought the same items as Julio before the sale. How much more did Nicolas pay for the items than Julio?

6. Read the clues, then work backward to find the number.

a. If you subtract 4.75 from the number and then add 1.75, you get 35. What is the number?

b. If you add 6.75 to the number and subtract 3.78 from the result, you get 8.75. What is the number?

CHAPTER 9 Angles

Lesson 9.1 Understanding and Measuring Angles

Name the angles in two ways.

1.

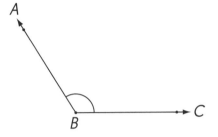

Angle at *B*: ∠_____ or ∠_____

2.

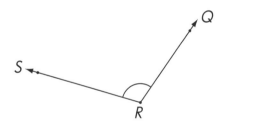

Angle at *R*: ∠_____ or ∠_____

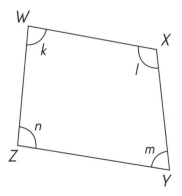

3. ∠*YZW*: ∠_____ or ∠_____

4. ∠*WXY*: ∠_____ or ∠_____

Name the angles in two ways.

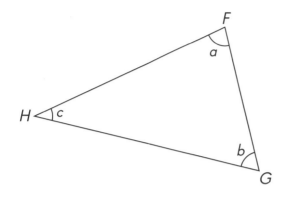

5. ∠FGH: ∠_____ or ∠_____

6. ∠GHF: ∠_____ or ∠_____

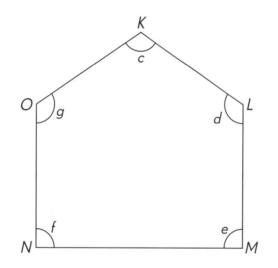

7. ∠OKL: ∠_____ or ∠_____

8. ∠NOK: ∠_____ or ∠_____

9. ∠LMN: ∠_____ or ∠_____

Decide which scale you would use to measure each angle.
Fill in the blanks with *inner scale* or *outer scale*.

10.

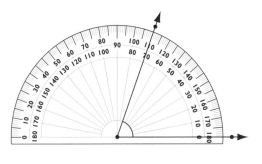

_____

11.

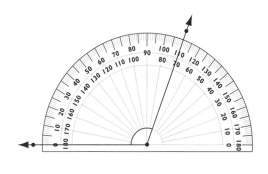

_____

12.

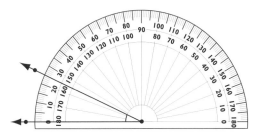

_____

13.

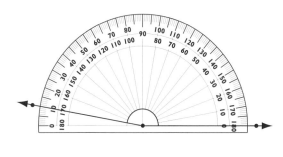

_____

14.

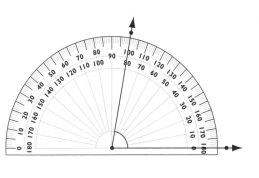

_____

15.

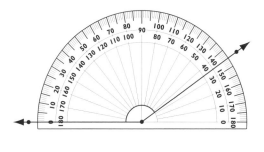

_____

Write the measure of each angle in degrees. State whether it is an
***acute angle* or an *obtuse angle*.**

16.

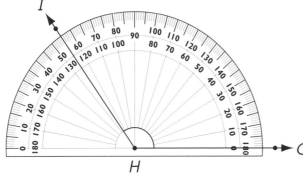

Measure of ∠GHI = _____

_____

17.

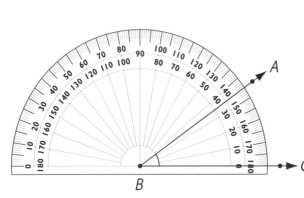

Measure of ∠ABC = _____

_____

18.

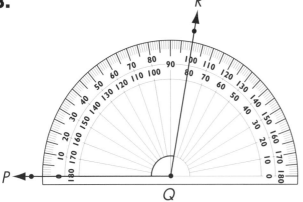

Measure of ∠PQR = _____

_____

Write the measure of the angle in degrees. State whether it is an
acute angle **or an** *obtuse angle***.**

19.

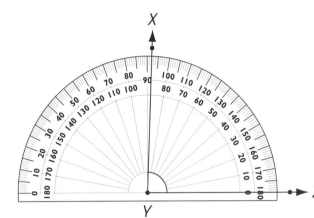

Measure of ∠XYZ = _____

_____

Estimate and then measure each angle.
Complete the table below.

20.

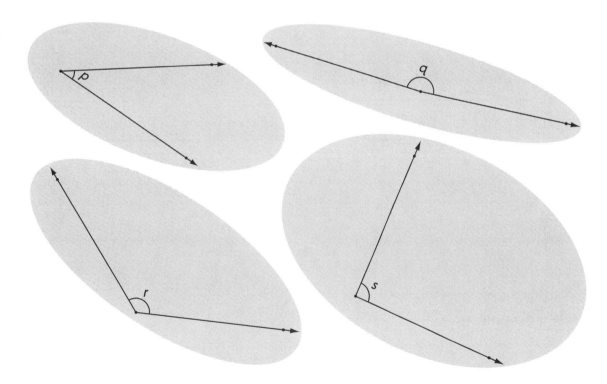

Angle	p	q	r	s
Estimate				
Measure				

Measure the marked angles.

21.

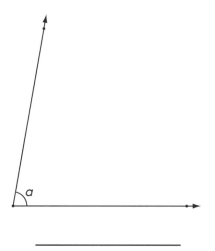

_____

22.

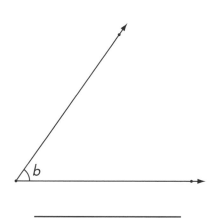

_____

23.

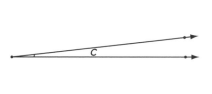

_____

24.

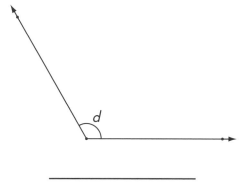

_____

25.

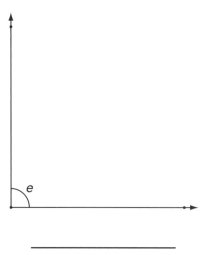

_____

26.

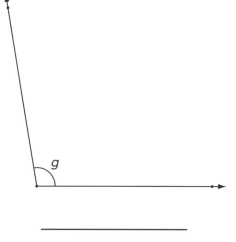

_____

Lesson 9.2   Drawing Angles to 180°

Use a protractor to draw each angle.

1.   57° using inner scale

2.   126° using outer scale

3.   64° using outer scale

4.   159° using inner scale

Draw a ray to form each angle.

5. $\angle ABC = 28°$

6. $\angle CDE = 89°$

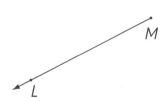

7. $\angle FGH = 96°$

8. $\angle LMN = 102°$

G

F

M

L

9. $\angle PQR = 74°$

10. $\angle XYZ = 135°$

Lesson 9.3   Turns and Right Angles

Fill in the blanks.

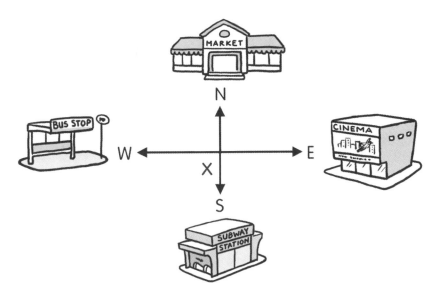

1.   You are at point X and you are facing the bus stop. You turn to the right until you

face the market. What fraction of a turn do you make? _____

2.   You are at point X and you are facing the cinema. You turn until you face the

bus stop. What fraction of a turn do you make? _____

3.   You are at point X and you are facing the subway station. You turn to the right

until you face the cinema. What fraction of a turn do you make? _____

4.   You are at point X and you are facing the market. You turn until you face

the market again. What angle do you turn through? _____

5.   You are at point X and you are facing the cinema. You turn to the right until you

face the market. What angle do you turn through? _____

**Use the diagram on the previous page to answer exercises 6 and 7.
Fill in the blanks.**

6. You are at point X and you are facing the bus stop. You turn to the left until you

    face the subway station. What angle do you turn through? _____

7. You are at point X and you are facing the subway station. You turn until you

    face the market. What angle do you turn through? _____

Solve. Draw diagrams to show the directions.

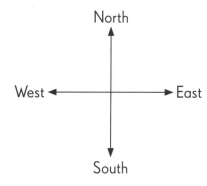

North

West ←———————→ East

South

8. Samantha is facing south. She makes a 90° turn to her right.
    Then she makes a $\frac{3}{4}$-turn to her left.

    Samantha ends up facing _____.

9. Dino starts by facing west. He makes a $\frac{3}{4}$-turn to his right.
    Then he makes a 180° turn.

    Dino ends up facing _____.

 Put on Your Thinking Cap!

Find the measure of each marked angle.

1.

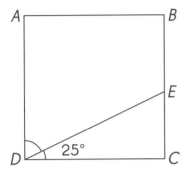

ABCD is a square.
The measure of ∠*CDE* = 25°

The measure of ∠*ADE* = _____

2.

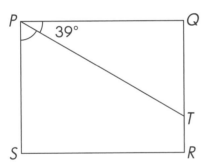

PQRS is a rectangle.
The measure of ∠*QPT* = 39°

The measure of ∠*SPT* = _____

3.

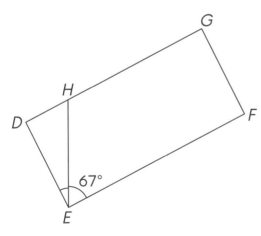

DEFG is a rectangle.
The measure of ∠*HEF* = 67°

The measure of ∠*DEH* = _____

4. How many right angles can you find in this figure?

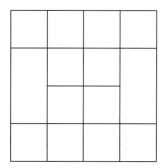

_____ right angles

Study the figures and then complete the table.

a.

b.

c.

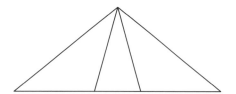

d.

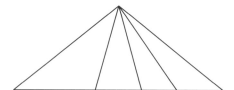

5.

Figures	Number of Angles Smaller than a Right Angle	Number of Angles Larger than a Right Angle
a.		
b.		
c.		
d.		

CHAPTER 10 Perpendicular and Parallel Line Segments

Lesson 10.1   Drawing Perpendicular Line Segments

Use a protractor to draw perpendicular line segments.

1. Draw a line segment perpendicular to $\overline{PQ}$ at point P.

2. Draw a line segment perpendicular to $\overline{RS}$ through point T.

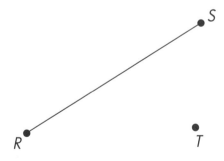

3. Draw a line segment perpendicular to $\overline{WX}$ at point Y.

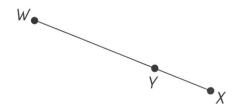

Use a drawing triangle to draw perpendicular line segments.

4. Draw a line segment perpendicular to $\overline{AB}$ through point C.

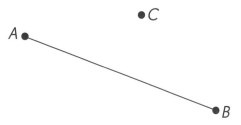

5. Draw a line segment perpendicular to $\overline{PQ}$ at point R.
Then draw another line segment perpendicular to $\overline{PQ}$ through point S.

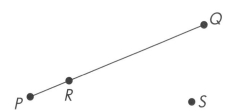

6. Draw a line segment perpendicular to $\overline{GH}$ at point H.
Label the line segment $\overline{FH}$. Then join points F and G.
What shape did you form? _____

Lesson 10.2   Drawing Parallel Line Segments

Use a drawing triangle and a straightedge to draw parallel line segments.

1.   Draw a line segment parallel to $\overline{CD}$ through point E.

2.   Draw a line segment parallel to $\overline{XY}$ through point V.

3.   Draw a line segment parallel to $\overline{PQ}$ through point R.

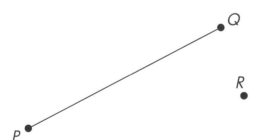

Use a drawing triangle and a straightedge to draw parallel line segments.

4. Draw a line segment parallel to $\overline{PQ}$ through point R.
Then draw another line segment parallel to $\overline{PQ}$
through point M. Are the two line segments you drew
parallel to each other? _____

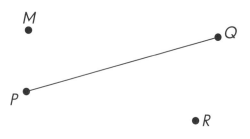

5. Draw a line segment parallel to $\overline{HG}$ at point F. Then draw
another line segment parallel to $\overline{FG}$ at point H. Extend
each line segment until they meet. What shape did you form?
_____

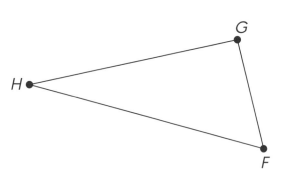

Lesson 10.3   Horizontal and Vertical Lines

Name the line segments in the given figures.

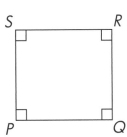
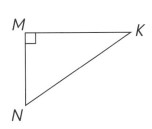

1.   The horizontal line segments are _____.

2.   The vertical line segments are _____.

3.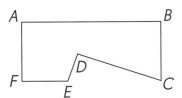

The horizontal line segments are _____.

The vertical line segments are _____.

4.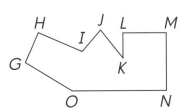

The horizontal line segments are _____.

The vertical line segments are _____.

Name the line segments in the given figure.

5.

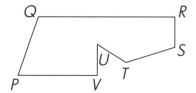

The horizontal line segments are _____.

The vertical line segments are _____.

Draw line segments. Then answer the question.

6. $\overline{AB}$ is a horizontal line segment. Draw a vertical line segment
at point B and label it $\overline{BC}$.

A •————————————————• B

7. $\overline{XY}$ is a vertical line segment.
Draw a horizontal line segment at point Y and label it $\overline{YZ}$.

X •

Y

8. What do you know about the relationship between vertical line
segments and horizontal line segments drawn on the same sheet of paper?

_____

_____

Put on Your Thinking Cap!

Use a protractor, or a drawing triangle and a straightedge, to name three pairs of line segments that are

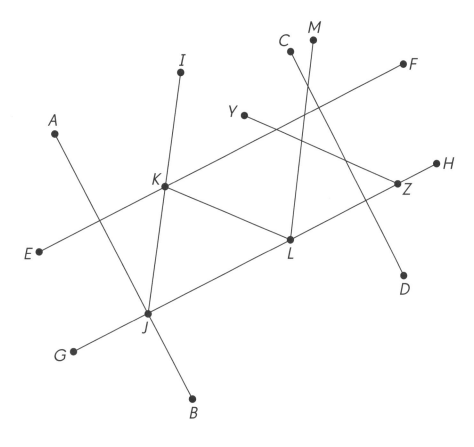

1. perpendicular: _____

    _____

2. parallel: _____

    _____

This is a map of Georgina's neighborhood.

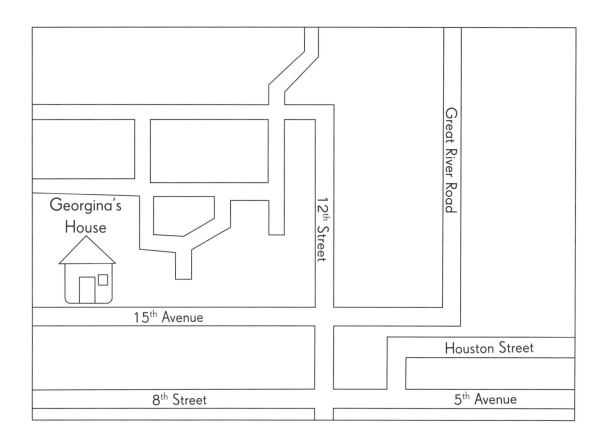

Fill in the blanks.

3. Which road is perpendicular to the road in front of

    Georgina's house and nearest to her house? _____

4. Name the roads that are parallel to 15th Avenue.

    _____

5. Name the four roads that are perpendicular to 12th Street.

    _____

Solve.

These figures are made from matchsticks. The number of right angles in each figure forms a pattern.

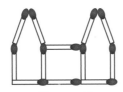
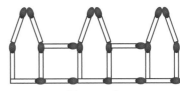

Figure 1   Figure 2   Figure 3

Figure 1 has 2 right angles.
Figure 2 has 8 right angles.
Figure 3 has 14 right angles.

6. Draw Figure 4 and state the number of right angles it has.

_____ right angles

7. How many right angles are there in Figure 6?
What is the pattern formed by the number of right angles?

_____ right angles

_____

Name: ____________________ Date: ____________________

Use the pattern you found on the previous page to complete the table.

8.

Figure Number	1	2	3	4	5	6	7	8	9	10
Number of Right Angles	2									

9. How many right angles will there be in the 20th figure?

____________________ right angles

10. State the number of right angles in the nth figure.

____________________ right angles

CHAPTER 11 Squares and Rectangles

Lesson 11.1 Squares and Rectangles

Study the figure. Then fill in the blanks.

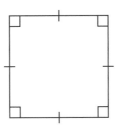

1. There are _____ right angles.

2. There are _____ equal sides.

3. There are _____ pairs of parallel sides.

4. The figure is a _____.

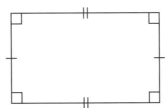

5. There are _____ right angles.

6. The opposite sides are _____.

7. There are _____ pairs of parallel sides.

8. The figure is a _____.

Study the figure. Then fill in the blanks.

$\overline{AB}$ is parallel to $\overline{CD}$.
$\overline{AC}$ is parallel to $\overline{BD}$.

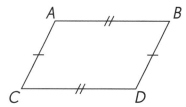

9. There are _____ right angles.

10. The opposite sides are _____.

11. There are _____ pairs of parallel sides.

12. Is this figure a rectangle? Why or why not?

_____

_____

$\overline{EF}$ is parallel to $\overline{HG}$.
$\overline{HE}$ is parallel to $\overline{GF}$.

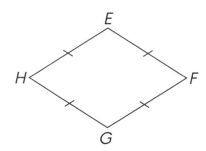

13. There are _____ right angles.

14. There are _____ equal sides.

15. There are _____ pairs of parallel sides.

16. Is this figure a square? Why or why not?

_____

_____

Study the figure. Then fill in the blanks.

$\overline{TU}$ is parallel to $\overline{WV}$.

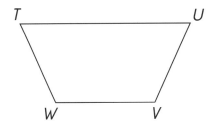

17. There are _____ right angles.

18. There is/are _____ pair(s) of parallel sides.

19. Is this figure a rectangle? Why or why not?

_____

_____

Find the unknown side lengths.

20. *ABCD* is a square.

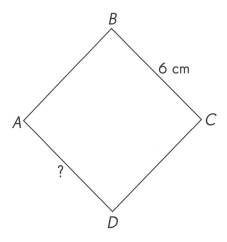

6 cm

?

$AD =$ _____ cm

21. *EFGH* is a rectangle.

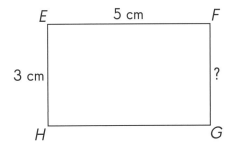

5 cm

3 cm

?

$FG =$ _____ cm

Find the unknown side lengths.

22.   *JKLM* is a rectangle. Its length is three times its width.

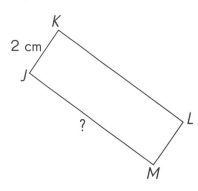

JM = _____ cm

23.   *ABCD* is a rectangle. Its shorter side is half the length of the longer side.

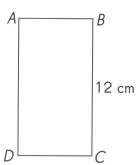

DC = _____ cm

Draw one line segment to divide each figure. Form two rectangles.

24.

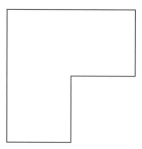

25.

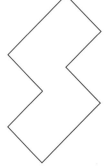

Draw one line segment to divide each figure. Form two rectangles.

26.

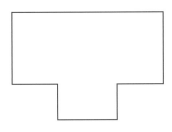

27.

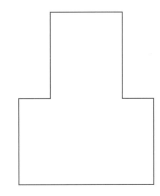

Draw one line segment to divide each figure.
Form one square and one rectangle.

28.

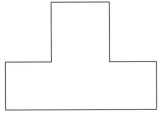

29.

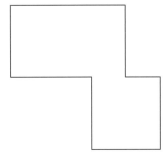

30.

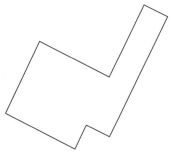

31.

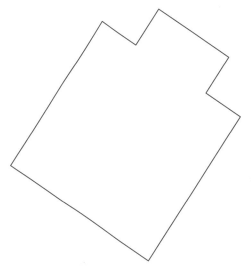

Draw two line segments to divide each figure.
Form two squares and one rectangle.

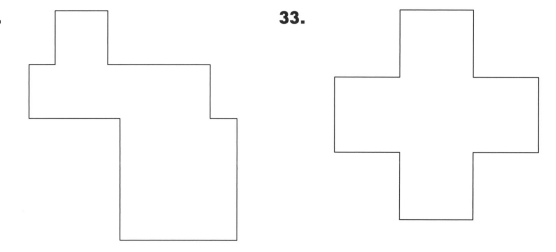

32.

33.

34.

Lesson 11.2   Properties of Squares and Rectangles

All the figures are rectangles.
Find the measure of the marked angles.

1.   Find the measure of ∠a.

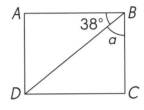

2.   Find the measure of ∠b.

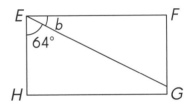

3.   Find the measure of ∠c.

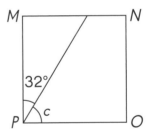

4.   Find the measure of ∠d.

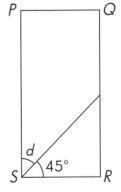

Find the lengths of the unknown sides.

5.   The figure is made up of three rectangles.
BC = DE. Find the length of $\overline{HG}$ and $\overline{DE}$.

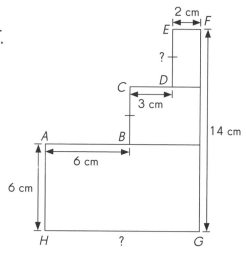

6.   The figure is made up of two rectangles.
Find the length of $\overline{ST}$ and $\overline{RS}$.

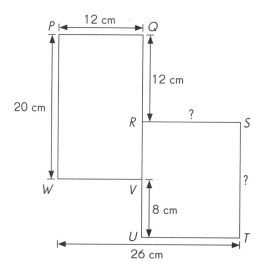

7.   The figure is made up of three rectangles.
Find the length of $\overline{AJ}$ and $\overline{HG}$.

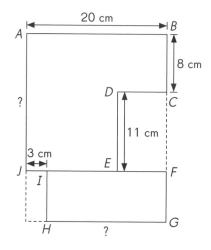

Put on Your Thinking Cap!

Solve.

1.   The figure is made up of small and big squares.
Find the total number of squares.

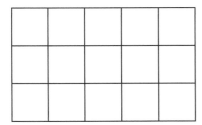

_____

2.   Look at the figure. What is the least number of rectangles that must
be added to the figure to make a square?

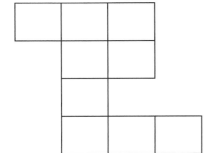

_____

3. The figure shows a square which is cut out of two identical overlapping rectangles. The length of each rectangle is three times the side width of the square. Find the width of each rectangle.

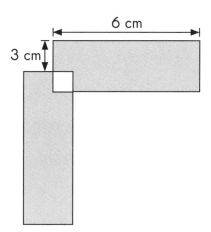

4. Draw line segments to divide the figure into three rectangles in three different ways.

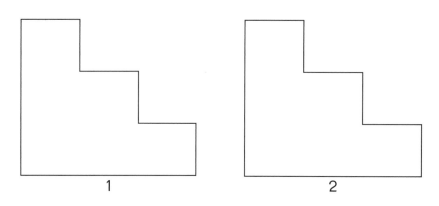

1   2

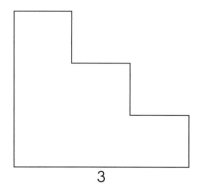

3

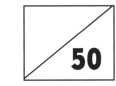

Test Prep

for Chapters 7 to 11

Multiple Choice (10 × 2 points = 20 points)

Fill the circle next to the correct answer.

1. In 483.52, the digit 2 stands for _____.

(A) 0.02   (B) 2   (C) 2 tenths   (D) hundredths

2. 129 hundredths is equal to _____.

(A) 0.129   (B) 1.29   (C) 12.90   (D) 129.0

3. Which of the following is the least number?

(A) $\frac{1}{4}$ (B) $\frac{3}{10}$ (C) 0.15   (D) 0.025

4. Express $2\frac{13}{20}$ as a decimal.

(A) 0.65   (B) 2.65   (C) 6.5   (D) 26.5

5. Find the sum of 6.88 and 3.98. Then round the sum to the nearest tenth. What number do you get?

(A) 10   (B) 10.8   (C) 10.86   (D) 10.9

6. Use a drawing triangle or a protractor to find the perpendicular line segments. Name the pair of perpendicular line segments in the diagram.

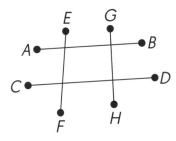

(A) $\overline{AB}$ and $\overline{CD}$

(B) $\overline{EF}$ and $\overline{GH}$

(C) $\overline{EF}$ and $\overline{CD}$

(D) $\overline{GH}$ and $\overline{AB}$

7. Use a drawing triangle and a straightedge to find the parallel line segments. How many pairs of parallel line segments are there in the figure?

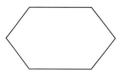

(A) 1   (B) 2   (C) 3   (D) 4

8. How many horizontal line segments are there in the figure?

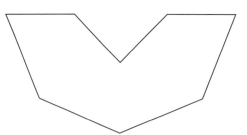

(A) 1   (B) 2   (C) 3   (D) 4

9. The figure is made up of squares and rectangles. How many right angles are there in the figure?

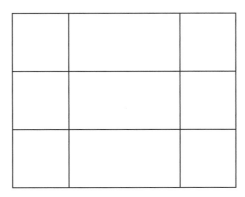

(A) 4   (B) 12   (C) 24   (D) 36

10. *PQRS* is a rectangle. The measure of $\angle TSR = 58°$. Find the measure of $\angle PST$.

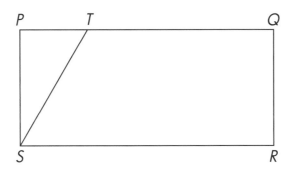

(A) 22°   (B) 32°   (C) 42°   (D) 58°

Short Answer (10 × 2 points = 20 points)

Write your answers in the space given.

11. Use a protractor, or a drawing triangle and a straightedge, to name one pair of parallel line segments and one pair of perpendicular line segments.

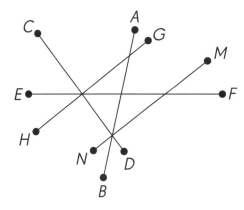

Answer: One pair of parallel line segments _____

Answer: One pair of perpendicular line segments _____

12. PQRS is a rectangle. The measure of ∠QPT = 35°. Find the measure of ∠SPT.

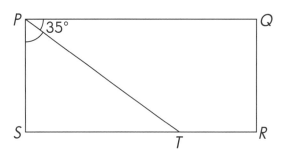

Answer: _____°

13.   *PQRS* is a square. Find the measure of ∠*x*.

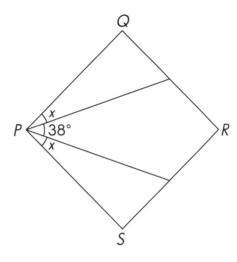

Answer: _____°

14.   What is the value of the digit 6 in 35.46?

Answer: _____

15.   Express 5.75 as a fraction in simplest form.

Answer: _____

16.   Continue the pattern.

2.78, 4.03, 5.78, 8.03, 10.78, ⬚

Answer: _____

17.   Subtract 1.54 from 5.12. Round your answer to the nearest tenth.

Answer: _____

18.   Express $3\frac{4}{5}$ as a decimal.

Answer: _____

19.   Maya is 143.6 centimeters tall. She is 9 centimeters taller than Rebecca. How tall is Rebecca?

Answer: _____ centimeters

20.   Devon buys a book for $8.75 and a file for $1.85. How much does Devon pay for both items?

Answer: $_____

Extended Response (10 points) (Questions 21 and 22: 3 points each)
(Question 23: 4 points)

Solve. Show your work.

21. I am thinking of a number. When I divide the number by 8 and subtract 34.7 from the result, I get 45.3. Find the number.

22. Nicole buys 10 meters of ribbon. She cuts off 1.88 meters of ribbon to tie a parcel and 2.45 meters of ribbon to tie a box. How many meters of ribbon does Nicole have left?

23. The total mass of Parcel A, Parcel B, and Parcel C is 14.2 kilograms. The total mass of Parcel A and Parcel B is 8.3 kilograms. The total mass of Parcel B and Parcel C is 10.7 kilograms. What is the mass of Parcel B?

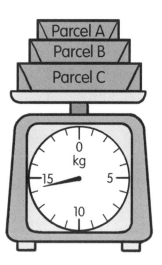

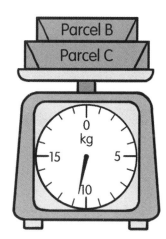

Area and Perimeter

Lesson 12.1 Area of a Rectangle

Find the area of each figure.

1.

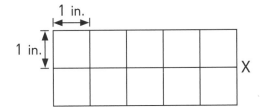

There are _____ rows of one-inch squares.

Each row has _____ one-inch squares.

_____ × _____ = _____

There are _____ one-inch squares covering Rectangle X.

Area of Rectangle X = _____ in.^{2}

2.

There is/are _____ row(s) of one-yard squares.

Each row has _____ one-yard squares.

_____ × _____ = _____

There are _____ one-yard squares covering Rectangle W.

Area of Rectangle W = _____ yd^2

3.

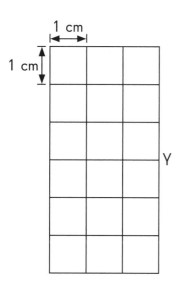

There are _____ rows of one-centimeter squares.

Each row has _____ one-centimeter squares.

_____ × _____ = _____

There are _____ one-centimeter squares covering Rectangle Y.

Area of Rectangle Y = _____ cm²

Complete to find the area of each figure.

4.

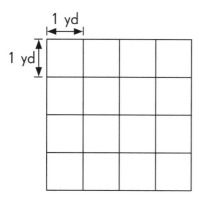

Area = length × width

= _____ × _____

= _____

The area is _____ square yards.

5.

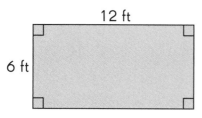

Area = _____ × _____

= _____

The area is _____ square feet.

Name: _____   Date: _____

Find the perimeter and area of each rectangle or square.

6.

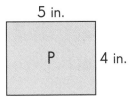
5 in.
P
4 in.

Perimeter = _____ in.

Area = _____ in.²

7.

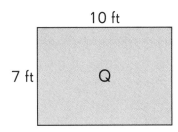
10 ft
7 ft
Q

Perimeter = _____ ft

Area = _____ ft²

8.

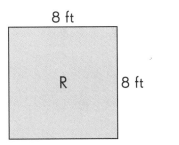
8 ft
R
8 ft

Perimeter = _____ ft

Area = _____ ft²

9.

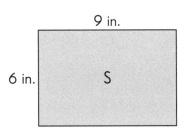
9 in.
6 in.
S

Perimeter = _____ in.

Area = _____ in.²

Solve.

10. A rectangular field measures 20 meters by 8 meters.
What is the area of the rectangular field?

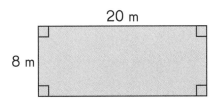
20 m
8 m

Solve.

11. James wants to put carpet in his living room.
     The living room measures 10 meters by 4 meters.
     What is the area of his living room?

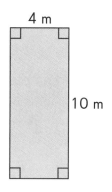

4 m

10 m

12. Helen has a piece of wrapping paper that measures 60 centimeters by
     9 centimeters. She uses half of it to wrap a birthday gift. What is the area
     of the piece of wrapping paper Helen has left?

Solve.

13. Four identical square tables are arranged next to each other to form one large rectangular table. The length of the large rectangular table is 12 feet. What is the area of each square table?

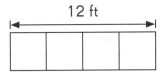

12 ft

14. A rectangular garden measures 15 meters by 22 meters. What is the cost of putting a fence around the garden if 1 meter of fencing costs $10?

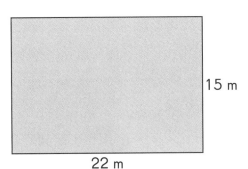

15 m

22 m

Estimate the area of each figure in square units.

15.

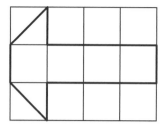

_____ unit²

16.

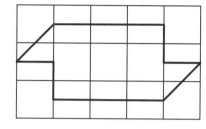

_____ unit²

17.

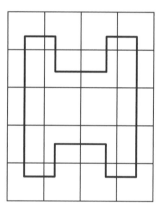

_____ unit²

18.

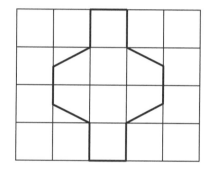

_____ unit²

19.

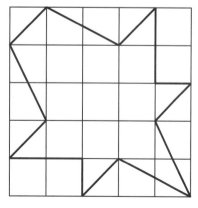

_____ unit²

20.

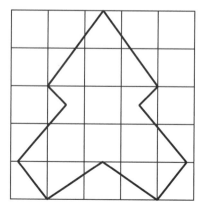

_____ unit²

Lesson 12.2   Rectangles and Squares (Part 1)

Find the perimeter of each figure.

1.   Perimeter of the rectangle

= _____ + _____ + _____ + _____

= _____

The perimeter of the rectangle is

_____ centimeters.

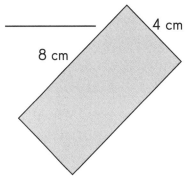

8 cm

4 cm

2.   Perimeter of the square

= 4 × _____

= _____

The perimeter of the square is

_____ inches.

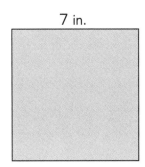

7 in.

Solve.

3.   A square piece of cardboard has a perimeter of 64 inches. Find the length
of one side of the cardboard.

? in

Perimeter = 64 in.

Solve.

4.   The perimeter of a square coaster is 40 centimeters.
Find the length of one side of the coaster.

Perimeter = 40 cm

? cm

5.   A rectangular shoe box has a width of 18 centimeters. Its perimeter is
100 centimeters. Find the length of the box.

Perimeter = 100 cm

? cm

18 cm

6.   A rectangular tray has a perimeter of 108 centimeters. Its length is
36 centimeters. Find the width of the tray.

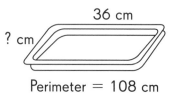

36 cm

? cm

Perimeter = 108 cm

Lesson 12.2   Rectangles and Squares (Part 2)

Find the area of each figure.

1.

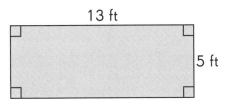

Area of the rectangle

= _____ × _____

= _____

The area of the rectangle is

_____ square feet.

2.

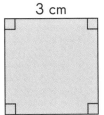

Area of the square

= _____ × _____

= _____

The area of the square is

_____ square centimeters.

Solve.

3.   The area of a rectangular field is 126 square yards. The width of the field is 9 yards. Find the length of the field.

? yd

Area = 126 yd²   9 yd

Solve.

4.   The area of a square is 81 square meters. Find the length of one side
      of the square.
      Hint: What number multiplied by itself is equal to 81?

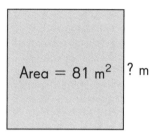

5.   The area of a square poster is 144 square centimeters.

      a.   Find the length of each side of the poster.

      b.   Find the perimeter of the poster.

6.   A rectangular photo frame has an area of 200 square centimeters. Its length
      is 20 centimeters.

      a.   Find the width of the photo frame.

      b.   Find the perimeter of the photo frame.

Solve.

7. The area of a rectangular piece of land is 240 square yards. Its width is 15 yards.

    a. Find the length of the land.

    b. Find the perimeter of the land.

8. The area of a square pond is 121 square meters.

    a. Find the length of one side of the pond.

    b. Find the perimeter of the pond.

Solve.

9.   The perimeter of a rectangle is 52 centimeters.
Its width is 10 centimeters.

    a.   Find the length of the rectangle.

    b.   Find the area of the rectangle.

10.   The perimeter of a rectangle is 54 inches. Its length is two times its width.

    a.   Find the length and width of the rectangle.

    b.   Find the area of the rectangle.

Lesson 12.3   Composite Figures

Find the lengths of the unknown sides of each figure.
Then find the perimeter of each figure.

1.

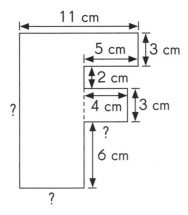

Length of first unknown side = _____ cm
Length of second unknown side = _____ cm
Length of third unknown side = _____ cm

Perimeter = _____ cm

2.

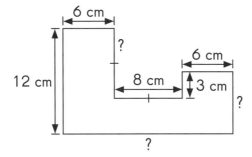

Length of first unknown side = _____ cm
Length of second unknown side = _____ cm
Length of third unknown side = _____ cm

Perimeter = _____ cm

Solve. Show your work.

3.

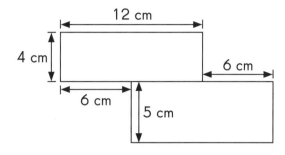

Perimeter = _____ cm

4.

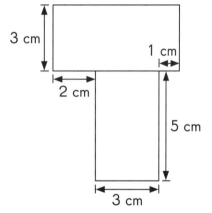

Perimeter = _____ cm

Find the area of each composite figure. Show your work.

5.   The figure is made up of a square *PQRS* and a rectangle *RSTU*.

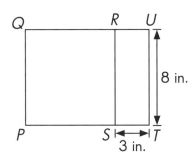

Area = _____ in.²

6.

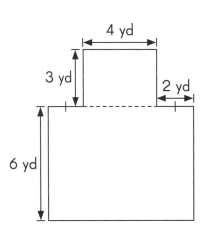

Area = _____ yd²

Find the area of each composite figure. Show your work.

7.

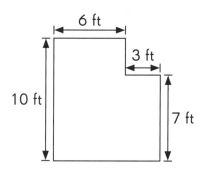

Area = _____ ft²

8.

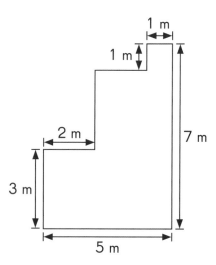

Area = _____ m²

Lesson 12.4   Using Formulas for Area and Perimeter

Solve. Show your work.

1.   A wall in Jason's room is in the shape shown below.

   a.   Estimate, in square meters, the area of the wall.

   b.   Jason wants to wallpaper his wall. A roll of wallpaper is 3 meters wide.
   What is the length of wallpaper Jason should buy?

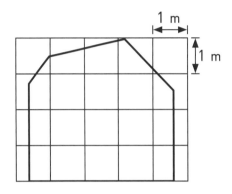

2.   A banner is in the shape shown below.

   a.   Estimate the banner's area.

   b.   Jamie wants to buy cloth to make the banner. One square meter
   of cloth costs $10. How much will Jamie have to spend?

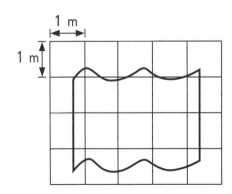

Name: _____   **Date:** _____

Solve. Show your work.

3. In the figure, the area of the shaded border is 87 square inches.
    Find the area of the large rectangle.

    Area of the small rectangle

    = _____ × _____

    = _____

    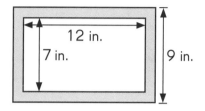

    Area of the large rectangle

    = Area of the small rectangle + area of the shaded border

    = _____ + _____

    = _____

    The area of the large rectangle is _____ square inches.

4. The border of a square garden has a width of 6 feet. What is the area
    of the shaded border?

    Area of the large square

    = _____ × _____

    = _____

    Area of the small square

    = _____ × _____

    = _____

    Area of the shaded border

    = _____ − _____

    = _____

    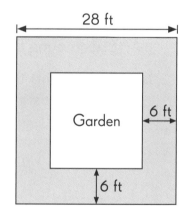

    The area of the shaded border is _____ square feet.

Solve. Show your work.

5. The area of the shaded part in the figure is 39 square meters.
    Find the area of the unshaded part of the figure.

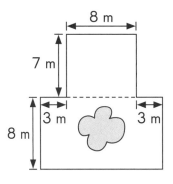

6. A rectangular field measuring 15 yards by 8 yards has a path 1 yard
    wide around it. Find the area of the path.

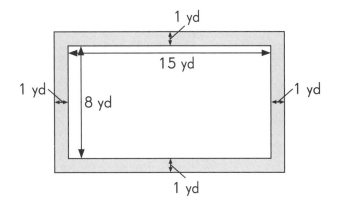

Solve. Show your work.

7. The figure is made up of five identical squares. The area of the figure is 405 square inches.

    a. Find the area of each square.

    b. Find the perimeter of the figure.

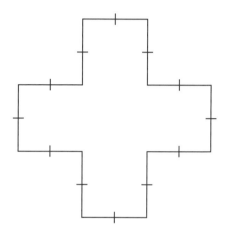

8. A coffee table is centered in a rectangular room as shown in the diagram.

    a. Find the area of the table.

    b. Find the perimeter of the room.

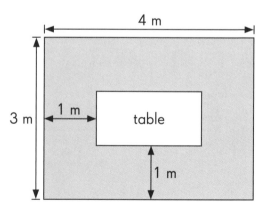

Put on Your Thinking Cap!

Solve. Show your work.

1. The figure is made up of two rectangles, A and B. The length of Rectangle A is $\frac{1}{4}$ the length of Rectangle B. The area of Rectangle B is 384 square inches.

a. Find the area of Rectangle A.

b. What is the perimeter of the figure?

8 in.	A	B Area = 384 in.²

2. The figure is made up of two identical large squares and four identical small squares. Each side of a large square is 9 inches long, while each side of a small square is 4 inches long. The shaded part is also a square. What is the area of the shaded square?

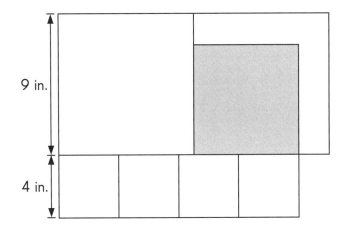

3. The figure is made up of 9 identical rectangles. The total area of the figure is 288 square centimeters. Find the perimeter of the figure.

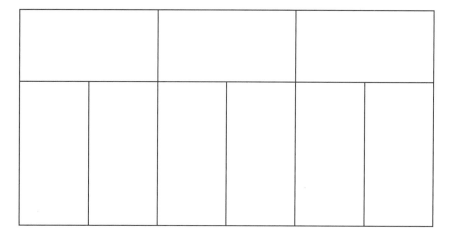

CHAPTER  Symmetry

Lesson 13.1   Identifying Lines of Symmetry

Is the dotted line in each figure a line of symmetry?
Write *Yes* or *No*.

1.

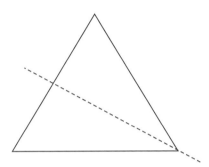

_____

2.

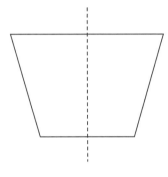

_____

3.

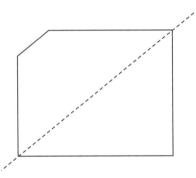

_____

4.

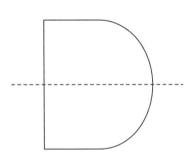

_____

5.

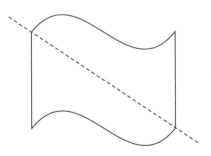

_____

6.

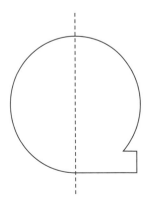

_____

Look at each figure. Which figures have lines of symmetry?
Write *Yes* or *No*.

7.

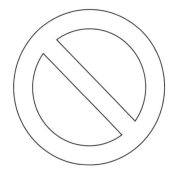

_____

8.

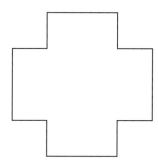

_____

9.

_____

10.

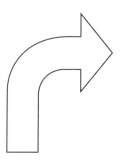

_____

11.

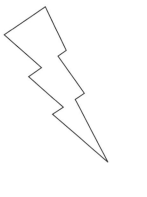

_____

12.

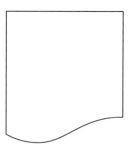

_____

Lesson 13.2   Rotational Symmetry

Decide whether each figure has rotational symmetry about the center shown. Write *Yes* or *No*.

1.

_____

2.

_____

3.

_____

4.

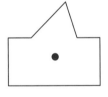

_____

5.

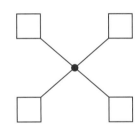

_____

6.

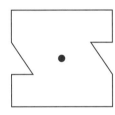

_____

7.

_____

8.

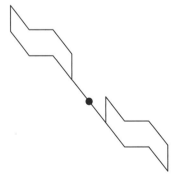

_____

Look at each figure. Which figures have rotational symmetry?
Write *Yes* or *No*.

9.

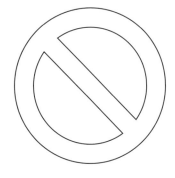

_____

10.

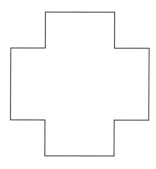

_____

11.

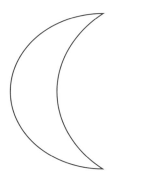

_____

12.

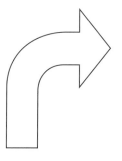

_____

13.

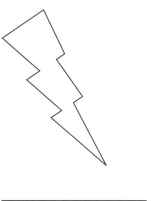

_____

14.

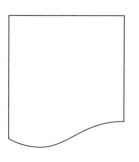

_____

Name: _____ Date: _____

Lesson 13.3   Making Symmetric Shapes and Patterns

Each figure below is half of a symmetric shape. The dotted line is a line of symmetry. Complete each symmetric figure.

1.

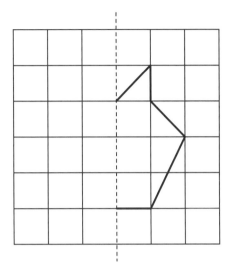

2.

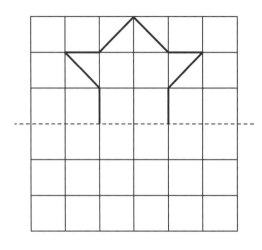

3.

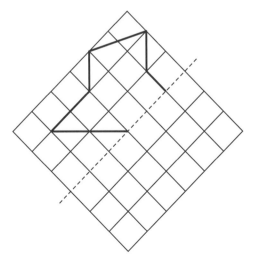

4.

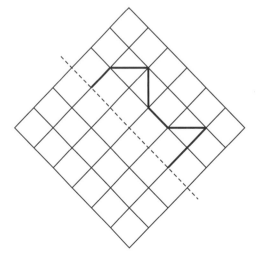

Name: _____   Date: _____

Each figure below is half of a symmetric shape. The dotted line is a line of symmetry. Complete each symmetric figure.

5.

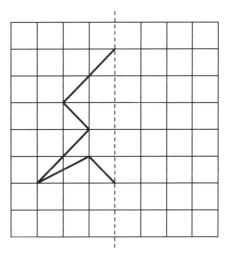

6.

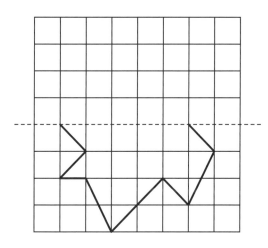

Shade the correct squares so that the pattern of shaded squares has line symmetry about the given dotted line.

7.

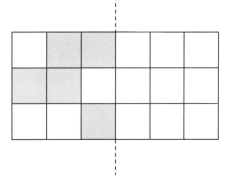

8.

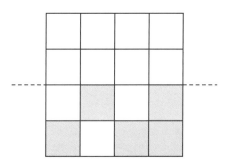

Shade five more squares in each figure so that the pattern of shaded squares has rotational symmetry about the given point.

9.

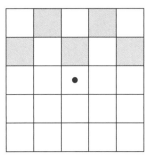

10.

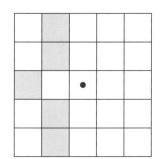

 **Put on Your Thinking Cap!**

Shade the correct squares or half-squares so that the pattern of shaded squares has line symmetry about the given dotted line.

1.

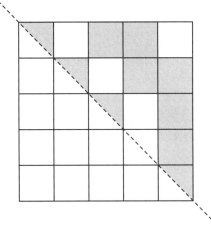

2.

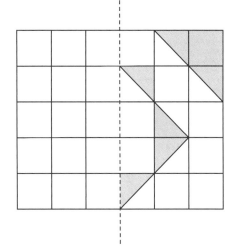

In the grid below, design a symmetric pattern with rotational symmetry about the given point.

3.

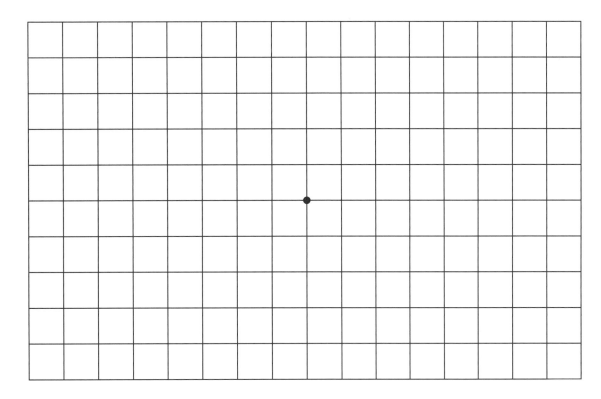

Do the shaded squares form a symmetric pattern? If they do, draw the line of symmetry.

4.

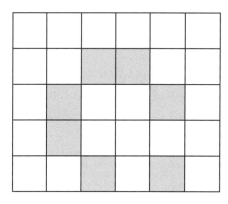

Shade the correct squares in each pattern so that it has line symmetry and rotational symmetry about the given point.

5.

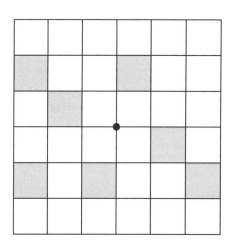

6.

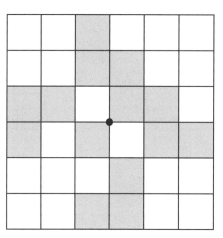

Name: _____   Date: _____

CHAPTER 14 Tessellations

Lesson 14.1   Identifying Tessellations

In each tessellation, color the repeated shape.

1.

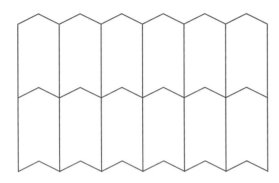

2.

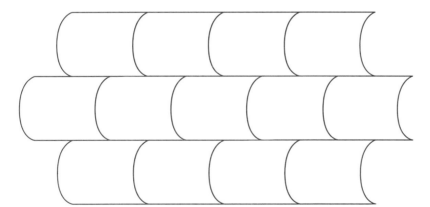

3.

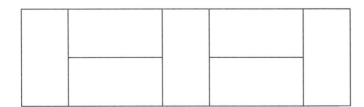

**Is each pattern a tessellation of a single repeated shape?
Write *Yes* or *No*. Explain your answer.**

4.

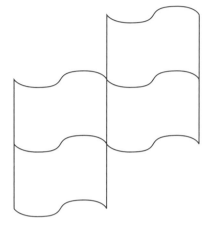

_____

_____

_____

_____

5.

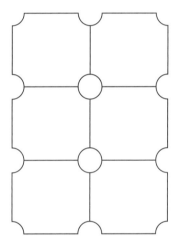

_____

_____

_____

_____

6.

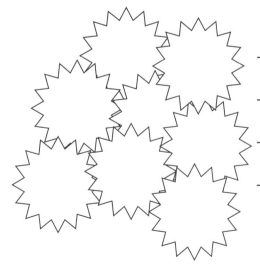

_____

_____

_____

_____

Add five more of the repeated shapes to the tessellation.

7.

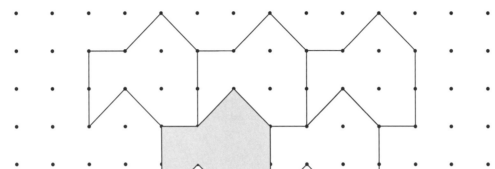

Add five more of the repeated shapes to the tessellation.

8.

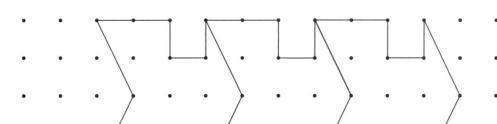

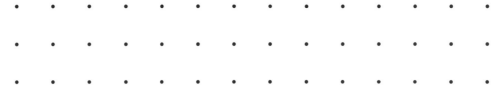

Use the shape to make a tessellation in the space provided.

9.

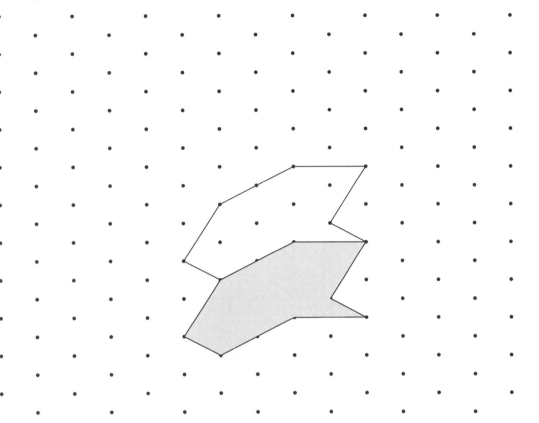

Use the shape to make a tessellation in the space provided.

10.

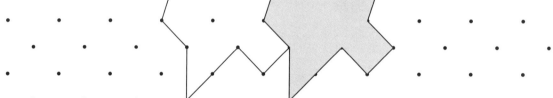

Use the shape to make a tessellation in the space provided.

11.

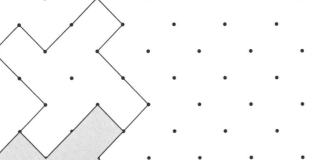

Use the shape to make a tessellation in the space provided.

12.

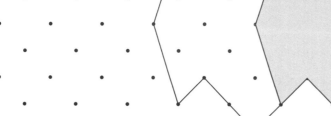

Use each shape to make a tessellation in the space provided.

13.   Tessellate this shape by rotating it.

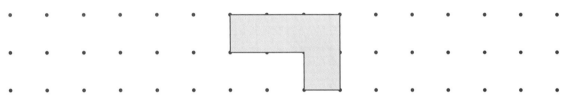

14. Tessellate this shape by rotating or flipping it.

Lesson 14.2   More Tessellations

Add five more of the repeated shapes to each tessellation.

1.   Tessellation 1

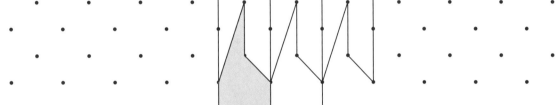
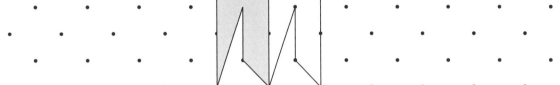

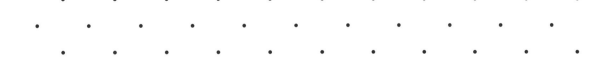

2. Tessellation 2

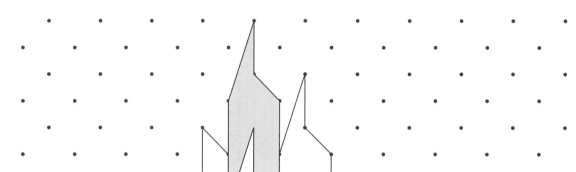

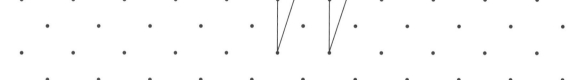

Use the shape to make two different tessellations in the space provided on this page and the next.

3.   Tessellation 1

4. Tessellation 2

Use a newly formed shape to make a tessellation.

From a square, the shaded parts are cut out and attached to different sides to form the final shape.

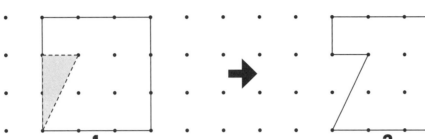

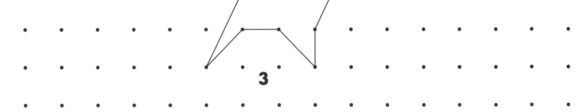

5. The new shape is shown on the dot grid below. Use this shape to make a tessellation in the space provided.

Put on Your Thinking Cap!

Design a new unit shape that can tessellate on the dot grid below.
Use two of these basic shapes to form the new unit shape:

Use your new shape to make tessellations on the grid.

1.

Joel draws a line across a rectangle and obtains two sections (Figure 1).
He draws two lines on a rectangle and obtains four sections (Figure 2).
He draws three lines on a rectangle to obtain the maximum number of
sections with three lines (Figure 3).

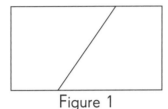
Figure 1

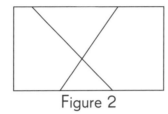
Figure 2

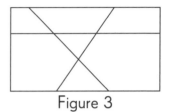
Figure 3

2. Using four lines, what is the maximum number of sections on the rectangle that
Joel can obtain? Complete Figure 4 to show the maximum number of sections.

Figure 4

Complete the following table.

3.

Number of Lines	Maximum Number of Sections Obtained	Pattern Observed	
1	2	$1 + 1 = 2$	$1 + \dfrac{1 \times 2}{2} = 2$
2	4	$1 + 1 + 2 = 4$	$1 + \dfrac{2 \times 3}{2} = 4$
3	7	$1 + 1 + 2 + 3 = 7$	$1 + \dfrac{3 \times 4}{2} = 7$
4			
5			
6			

End-of-Year Test

100

Multiple Choice (20 × 2 points = 40 points)

Fill in the circle next to the correct answer.

1. Which figure does not have a pair of parallel line segments?

(A) trapezoid   (B) rhombus   (C) pentagon   (D) rectangle

2. Use a protractor, or a drawing triangle and a straightedge, to find the perpendicular line segments. Which line segment is perpendicular to line segment *AB*?

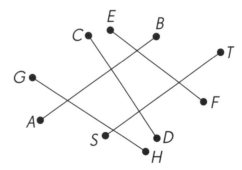

(A) $\overline{CD}$ (B) $\overline{EF}$ (C) $\overline{GH}$ (D) $\overline{ST}$

3. Name a pair of horizontal line segments in the diagram.

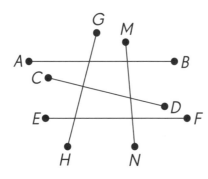

Ⓐ $\overline{AB}$ and $\overline{CD}$

Ⓑ $\overline{GH}$ and $\overline{MN}$

Ⓒ $\overline{AB}$ and $\overline{EF}$

Ⓓ $\overline{MN}$ and $\overline{EF}$

4. Which of the figures does not have a line of symmetry?

Ⓐ

Ⓑ

Ⓒ

Ⓓ

5. Which of the dotted line segments is a line of symmetry?

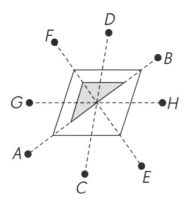

Ⓐ $\overline{AB}$ Ⓑ $\overline{CD}$ Ⓒ $\overline{EF}$ Ⓓ $\overline{GH}$

6. Round 18,949 to the nearest hundred.

(A) 18,900   (B) 18,940   (C) 18,950   (D) 19,000

7. The length of Lincoln Road is 12.576 kilometers. Round the distance to the nearest kilometer.

(A) 10 km   (B) 12.58 km   (C) 12.6 km   (D) 13 km

8. Which one of the following is the best estimate of 597 $\times$ 42?

(A) 20,000   (B) 22,000   (C) 24,000   (D) 30,000

9. Which of these numbers is greatest?

(A) 2.45   (B) 2.54   (C) $2\frac{11}{20}$ (D) $2\frac{49}{100}$

10. I am thinking of a fraction. I subtract $\frac{1}{6}$ from it. Then I add $\frac{3}{4}$ to the difference. The answer is $\frac{5}{4}$. What is the fraction?

(A) $1\frac{5}{6}$ (B) $1\frac{5}{12}$ (C) $\frac{2}{3}$ (D) $\frac{1}{3}$

11. The numbers in each circle are multiples of a number. Find the number that belongs in the box.

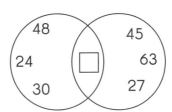

(A) 36   (B) 60   (C) 62   (D) 96

12. Find the perimeter of the figure. All the angles are right angles.

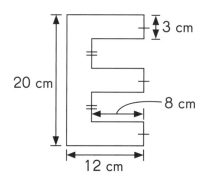

(A) 53 cm   (B) 61 cm   (C) 64 cm   (D) 96 cm

13. The length of a rectangle is two times its width. The width is 8 centimeters. What is the area of the rectangle?

(A) 32 cm²   (B) 96 cm²   (C) 128 cm²   (D) 144 cm²

14. The figure below is made up of square *ABCD* and rectangle *CDEF*.

The perimeter of the figure is _____.

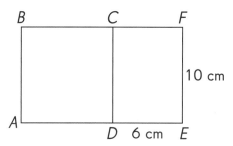

(A) 32 cm   (B) 40 cm   (C) 52 cm   (D) 160 cm

15. Which of these shapes can form tessellation(s)?

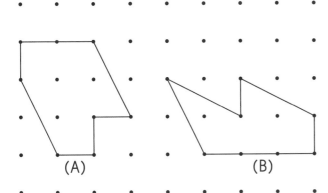 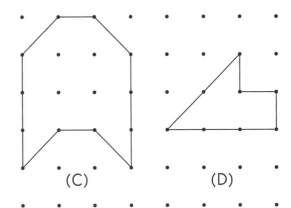

(A)   (B)   (C)   (D)

(A) A, B, and C only

(B) B, C, and D only

(C) A, C, and D only

(D) A, B, C, and D

16. Write 306 hundredths as a decimal.

(A) 30.6   (B) 3.06   (C) 0.306   (D) 0.036

17. Find the sum of 31 tenths and 428 hundredths.

(A) 738 hundredths

(B) 738 tenths

(C) 73.8

(D) 738

18. Mrs. Keysers bought seven identical T-shirts for $69.65.
Round $69.65 to the nearest tenth.

(A) $70   (B) $69   (C) $69.60   (D) $69.70

19.   Find the area of the shaded figure.

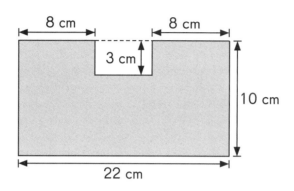

(A)   160 cm²   (B)   178 cm²   (C)   202 cm²   (D)   220 cm²

20.   Find the perimeter of the given figure.

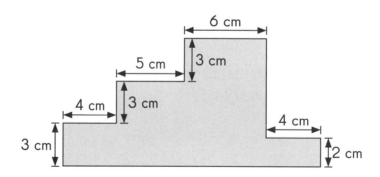

(A)   42 cm   (B)   48 cm   (C)   52 cm   (D)   56 cm

Short Answer (20 × 2 points = 40 points)

Write your answer in the space given.

21. Write the decimals in order from greatest to least.

20.06 21.60 20.60 21.06

Answer: _____

22. Find the median and mode of the set of numbers:

30, 22, 25, 28, 27, 23, 27, 24

Answer: **a.** Median _____

b. Mode _____

23. A card is drawn from a set of 15 cards that have the numbers 1 through 15 on them. What is the probability of drawing a card that is a multiple of 3?

Answer: _____

24. Use a protractor to draw an angle that has a measure of 138° using the inner scale.

25. Use a protractor or drawing triangle to draw a line segment perpendicular to $\overline{HI}$ through point Y. Label the line segment $\overline{YZ}$.

26. Continue the number pattern.

16.25   16.5   16.4   16.65   16.55 _____ 16.7

Answer: _____

27. In the figure below, the dotted line segment is a line of symmetry. Shade the correct squares and half-squares on the other side to make a symmetric pattern.

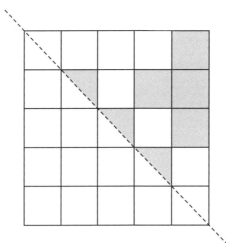

28. Express $6\frac{3}{8}$ as a decimal correct to 2 decimal places.

Answer: _____

29. In the figure, the area of square *ABCD* is 4 times the area of the square *CEFG*. What is the area of the figure?

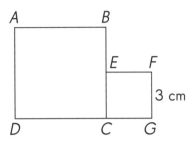

Answer: _____ centimeters²

Shade the correct squares on the other side so that the pattern of shaded squares has line symmetry with the dotted line as a line of symmetry.

30.

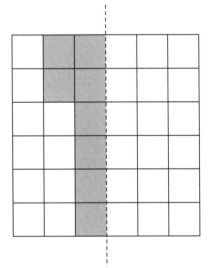

31.

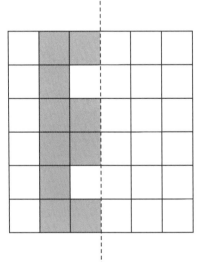

Shade the correct squares on the other side so that the pattern of shaded squares has line symmetry with the dotted line as a line of symmetry.

32.

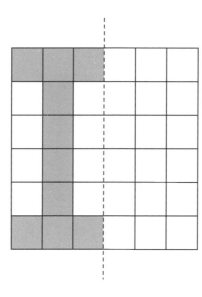

33. Gina has a piece of cardboard measuring 90 centimeters by 64 centimeters. She wants to cut out 6-centimeter squares from the piece of cardboard. What is the maximum number of squares that Gina can cut from the cardboard?

Answer: _____ squares

34. How many right angles are there in $\frac{3}{4}$ of a complete turn?

Answer: _____

35. There are 128 marbles in a box. Of the marbles in the box, $\frac{5}{8}$ of them are blue and the rest are green. How many green marbles are there in the box?

Answer: _____ green marbles

36. *ABCD* is a rectangle and the measure of ∠*BCE* = 46°. Find the measure of ∠*DCE*.

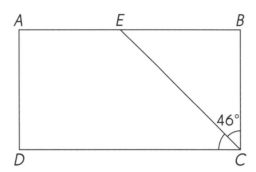

Answer: _____°

Study the graph and answer questions 37 through 39.

The graph shows the number of toy cars owned by six children.

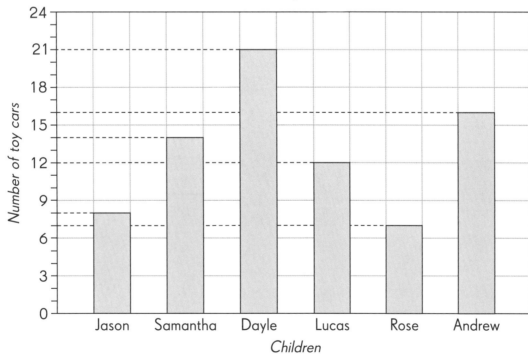

37. Andrew has 2 times as many toy cars as _____.

Answer: _____

38. The child with the greatest number of toy cars has _____ more toy cars than the child with the least number of toy cars.

Answer: _____

39. If all the children share the toy cars equally, how many toy cars will each child have?

Answer: _____ toy cars

Use the shape to make a tessellation in the space provided.

40. Add six more of the repeated shapes to the tessellation.

Extended Response (5 × 4 points = 20 points)

Solve. Show your work.

41. Ann, Brian, and Cindy share 544 beads. Ann has 56 more beads than Brian. Cindy has 34 fewer beads than Brian. How many beads does Ann have?

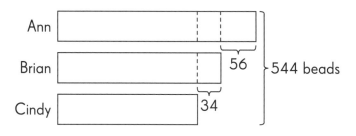

42. *ABCD* is a rectangle and *DCEF* is a square. The perimeter of square *DCEF* is 24 centimeters. The perimeter of rectangle *ABCD* is 42 centimeters. Find the length of rectangle *ABCD*.

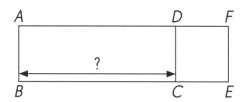

43. The rectangle has the same perimeter as the square. Find the area of the rectangle.

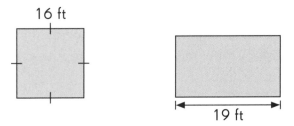

16 ft

19 ft

44. A rectangular garden measuring 23 meters by 18 meters is surrounded by a 1-meter wide path as shown in the diagram.

a. Find the area of the path.

b. It costs $27 to cement 1 square meter of the path. What is the cost of cementing the whole path?

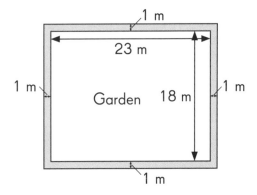

1 m

23 m

1 m   Garden   18 m   1 m

1 m

45. In the figure, the length of each of the two squares is a 1-digit whole number. The total perimeter of the two squares is 52 centimeters. Find a possible area of the shaded part.

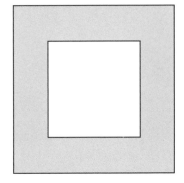

© Marshall Cavendish International (Singapore) Private Limited.

Answers

Chapter 7

Lesson 7.1

1. 0.4; 0.6
2. 0.7; 0.3
3. 0.9; 0.1
4. 1.2; 0.8
5. 1.6; 0.4
6. 2.1; 0.9
7. 0.9
8. 3.2

9.
```
 +--+--+--+--+--+--+--+--+--+--+--+--+--+--+--+--+--+--+--+
 0        1.0       2.0       3.0       4.0
        ↑   ↑           ↑      ↑        ↑
      [0.7][1.3]      [2.4]  [3.1]    [3.8]
```

10.
```
 +--+--+--+--+--+--+--+--+--+--+--+--+--+--+--+--+--+--+--+
 0      2.0       4.0       6.0             8.0
    ↑      ↑        ↑        ↑           ↑
  [0.4]  [1.8]    [3.6]    [5.0]       [7.2]
```

11. 0.4
12. 2.5
13. 6.8
14. 17.6
15. 3.9
16. 40.2
17. 0.6
18. 0.9
19. 4.8
20. 7.2
21. 16.1
22. 44.5
23. 6.3
24. 5.0 or 5
25. 21.0 or 21
26. 20.1
27. 30.0 or 30
28. 33.0 or 33

Number of Tenths	Fraction	Decimal
29. 6 tenths	$\frac{6}{10}$	0.6
30. 19 tenths	$1\frac{9}{10}$	1.9
31. 57 tenths	$5\frac{7}{10}$	5.7
32. 124 tenths	$12\frac{4}{10}$	12.4
33. 203 tenths	$20\frac{3}{10}$	20.3
34. 455 tenths	$45\frac{5}{10}$	45.5

35. $3\frac{7}{10}$; 3.7
36. $1\frac{9}{10}$; 1.9
37. $1\frac{3}{10}$; 1.3
38. 9
39. <u>6</u> ones
40. <u>2</u> tenths
41. <u>5</u> tens
42. <u>9</u> tens <u>0</u> ones
43. $5 + \frac{2}{10}$
44. $10 + 6 + \frac{3}{10}$
45. 8 + 0.4
46. 70 + 0 + 0.9

47. tenths; 0.7
48. ones; 8
49. 6; 60
50. 4; 0.4

Lesson 7.2

1. 0.16; 0.84
2. 0.05; 0.95
3. 0.89; 0.11
4. 1.2; 0.8
5. 1.06; 0.94
6. 2.03, 0.97
7. 0.53
8. 3.08

9.
```
 +--+--+--+--+--+--+--+--+--+--+--+--+--+--+--+--+--+--+--+
 0        0.1       0.2       0.3         0.4
      ↑      ↑        ↑         ↑       ↑
    [0.05] [0.12]   [0.19]    [0.26]  [0.33]
```

10.
```
 +--+--+--+--+--+--+--+--+--+--+--+--+--+--+--+--+--+--+--+
 0       0.2       0.4       0.6         0.8
      ↑     ↑        ↑        ↑          ↑
    [0.14][0.26]   [0.38]   [0.5]      [0.72]
```

11. 0.09
12. 0.10
13. 0.35
14. 2.06
15. 0.86
16. 41.03
17. 50.22
18. 0.04
19. 0.19
20. 0.65
21. 0.8
22. 2.14
23. 15.03
24. 30.08
25. 1.69
26. 2.02
27. 2.5
28. <u>8</u> hundredths
29. <u>25</u> hundredths
30. <u>40</u> hundredths
31. <u>607</u> hundredths
32. <u>539</u> hundredths
33. <u>980</u> hundredths

Number of Hundredths	Fraction	Decimal
34. 1 hundredths	$\frac{1}{100}$	0.01
35. 6 hundredths	$\frac{6}{100}$	0.06
36. 9 hundredths	$\frac{9}{100}$	0.09
37. 13 hundredths	$\frac{13}{100}$	0.13
38. 59 hundredths	$\frac{59}{100}$	0.59
39. 106 hundredths	$1\frac{6}{100}$	1.06

40. 7 tenths; 5 hundredths

41. 3 ones; 6 hundredths

42. 8 hundredths

43. 6 ones; 2 tenths; 3 hundredths

44. 9 ones; 5 tenths; 0 hundredths

45. $1 + \frac{5}{10} + \frac{6}{100}$

46. $20 + 4 + 0 + \frac{7}{100}$

47. 3 + 0.8 + 0.09

48. 50 + 1 + 0.5 + 0.02

49. hundredths; 0.03

50. tenths; 0

51. 6; 60   52. 2; 0.02

53. $0.35   54. $0.70

55. $1.08   56. $2.40

57. $6.35   58. $9.05

Lesson 7.3 (Part 1)

1. 2.0   2. 1.4

3. 1.9   4. 1.2

5. 1.6   6. 1.27

7. 1.25   8. 1.29

9. 1.23   10. 1.21

11. 1.08; 1.10
    1.06 + 0.02 = 1.08
    1.08 + 0.02 = 1.10

12. 5.15; 6.35
    3.95 + 1.2 = 5.15
    5.15 + 1.2 = 6.35

13. 4.96; 4.64
    5.28 − 0.32 = 4.96
    4.96 − 0.32 = 4.64

14. 4.35; 3.15
    5.55 − 1.2 = 4.35
    4.35 − 1.2 = 3.15

15. 6.32; 6.26
    6.28 + 0.04 = 6.32
    6.22 + 0.04 = 6.26

Lesson 7.3 (Part 2)

1. 2.06 is greater than 2.03.

2. 0.32 is less than 0.35.

3. 8.32 is greater than 8.23.

4. 0.09 is less than 0.90.

5. <

6. <

7. <

8. >

9. greatest: 0.54; least: 0.15

10. greatest: 7.86; least: 6.78

11. 0.68; 0.82; 0.86

12. 0.89; 0.98; 0.99

13. 0.57; 0.70; 0.75

14. 5.46; 5.64; 6.54

15. 0.10; 0.09; 0.07

16. 0.99; 0.90; 0.09

17. 3.08; 0.83; 0.38

18. 9.48; 8.94; 8.49

Lesson 7.4 (Part 1)

1. 6; 6

2. 2; 2

3. 130.7 centimeters is about 131 centimeters.

4. 5.95 liters is about 6 liters.

5. 1.8 pounds is about 2 pounds.

6. 2.49 kilometers is about 2 kilometers.

7. $39.59 is about 40 dollars.

Lesson 7.4 (Part 2)

1. 3.1; 3.1

2. 13.1; 13.1

3. 2.05 pounds is about 2.1 pounds.

4. 1.34 meters is about 1.3 meters.

5. 15.59 kilometers is about 15.6 kilometers.

6. 3.46 liters is about 3 liters.

7. 96.52 pounds is about 97 pounds.

8. 1; 0.7

9. 1; 1.3

10. 3; 3.1

11. 9; 8.7

12. 19; 19.5

13. 24; 24.0

14. 36; 36.2

15. 42; 42.0

Lesson 7.5

1. 0.4	2. 0.67
3. 0.3	4. 0.49
5. 5.9	6. 8.79
7. 2; 0.2	8. 38; 0.38
9. 0.8	10. 0.5
11. 1.75	12. 0.3
13. 0.64	14. 7.2
15. $\frac{3}{5}$	16. $5\frac{7}{10}$
17. $1\frac{9}{20}$	18. $3\frac{9}{25}$

Put on Your Thinking Cap!

1.

2.

3. Accept any number from 5.31 to 5.39.
4. Accept any number from 0.41 to 0.49.
5. Accept any number from 3.86 to 3.94.

6. 83	7. 258
8. 370	9. 56
10. 182	11. 394

12. a. 9
    b. 9.0
13. 12.98
    pattern: $+ 2.2$; $+ 2.2$; $+ 2.2$; $+ 2.2$; $+ 2.2$
14. 1.6
    pattern: $- 0.04$; $- 0.04$; $- 0.04$; $- 0.04$; $- 0.04$
15. 8.7
    pattern: $+ 0.5$; $+ 1.0$; $+ 1.5$; $+ 2.0$; $+ 2.5$
16. 0.7
    pattern: $- 0.2$; $- 0.4$; $- 0.6$; $- 0.8$; $- 1.0$
17. 1.68
    pattern: $+ 0.01$; $+ 0.01$; $- 0.02$; $- 0.02$; $+ 0.01$; $+ 0.01$
18. 0.42
    pattern: $- 0.3$; $- 0.6$; $- 0.9$; $- 1.2$; $- 1.5$
19. 12.38
    pattern: $- 0.4$; $+ 1.4$; $- 0.8$; $+ 2.8$; $- 1.2$; $+ 4.2$

Chapter 8

Lesson 8.1 (Part 1)

1. 1.9
2. 5; 7; 12; 1.2
3. 14; 23; 37; 3.7
4. 10.8
5. 32.9
6. 45.4
7. 23.2
8. 35.4
9. 33
10. 30.5
11. 40

Lesson 8.1 (Part 2)

1. 1.79
2. 71; 29; 100; 1.00
3. 38; 15; 53; 0.53
4. 65; 45; 110; 1.10
5. $30.99
6. $22.17
7. $44.34
8. $57.27
9. $0.59
10. $1.22
11. $1.36
12. $1.43

Lesson 8.2

1. 1.32
2. 25; 8; 17; 1.7
3. 34; 9; 25; 2.5
4. 32; 17; 15; 0.15
5. 21; 7; 14; 0.14
6. 0.63
7. 0.45
8. 0.29
9. 0.7
10. 3.9
11. 4.9
12. 8.34

13. 14.52

14. 11.09

15. 18.76

Lesson 8.3

1. $0.55 + 1.08 = 1.63$
   $2.50 - 1.63 = 0.87$
   0.87 pound of potatoes are left.

2. $\$4.95 + \$7.85 = \$12.80$
   $\$50.00 - \$12.80 = \$37.20$
   Ms. Petrie has $37.20 left.

3. $58.5 - 29.7 = 28.8$
   $71.4 - 28.8 = 42.6$
   The weight of Container A is 42.6 pounds.

4. $1.04 + 0.24 = 1.28$ (Paul)
   $1.28 - 0.16 = 1.12$
   Royston jumps 1.12 meters.

5. a. $7.49 + 9.87 = 17.36$
   John travels 17.36 kilometers.
   b. $17.36 + 9.87 = 27.23$
   John travels a total of 27.23 kilometers.

6. $60 - 45.8 = 14.20$
   a. The short stick is 14.20 centimeters shorter than the long stick.
   b. 3.6 m = 360 cm
   The length of the tail is 360 centimeters.
   $60 \times 6 = 360$ cm
   6 long sticks put end to end will be as long as the tail.

Put on Your Thinking Cap!

1. 7.37
   $8.97 + 3.68 = 12.65$
   $20.02 - 12.65 = 7.37$

2. Andy has $8.75 more than Calvin.

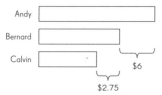

   $\$6 + \$2.75 = \$8.75$

3. $\$2.30 - \$1.95 = \$0.35$
   Amount saved by buying 1 ballpoint pen on sale: $0.35
   $\$0.35 + \$0.35 + \$0.35 = \$1.05$
   Amount saved by buying 3 ballpoint pens on sale is $1.05.

4. $\$0.85 + \$0.85 + \$2.75 = \$4.45$
   $\$10.00 - \$4.45 = \$5.55$
   The amount of change Julio gets back is $5.55.

5. $\$1.20 - \$0.85 = \$0.35$
   A mechanical pencil costs $0.35 more before the sale.
   $\$3.50 - \$2.75 = \$0.75$
   A correction pen costs $0.75 more before the sale.
   $\$0.35 + \$0.35 + \$0.75 = \$1.45$
   Nicolas paid $1.45 more than Julio.

6. a. $35.00 - 1.75 = 33.25$
   $33.25 + 4.75 = 38$
   The number is 38.
   b. $8.75 + 3.78 = 12.53$
   $12.53 - 6.75 = 5.78$
   The number is 5.78.

Chapter 9

Lesson 9.1

1. $\angle ABC$; $\angle CBA$

2. $\angle QRS$; $\angle SRQ$

3. $\angle n$; $\angle WZY$

4. $\angle l$; $\angle YXW$

5. $\angle b$; $\angle HGF$

6. $\angle c$; $\angle FHG$

7. $\angle c$; $\angle LKO$

8. $\angle g$; $\angle KON$

9. $\angle e$; $\angle NML$

10. inner scale

11. outer scale

12. outer scale

13. inner scale

14. inner scale

15. outer scale

16. 125°; obtuse angle

17. 35°; acute angle

18. 100°; obtuse angle

19. 88°; acute angle

20. Estimates will vary.

Angle	p	q	r	s
Measured $\angle$	37°	175°	128°	90°

Questions 21 to 26:

Accept any answer that is −1° or +1° from these answers.

21. 80°
22. 54°
23. 5°
24. 120°
25. 90°
26. 100°

Lesson 9.2

1.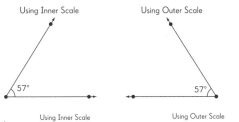

Using Inner Scale   Using Outer Scale

57°   57°

2.
Using Inner Scale   Using Outer Scale

126°   126°

3.
Using Inner Scale   Using Outer Scale

64°   64°

4.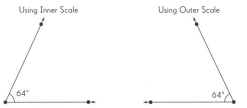
Using Inner Scale   Using Outer Scale

159°   159°

5.

OR

6.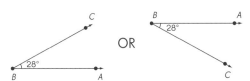

OR

7.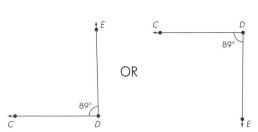

OR

8.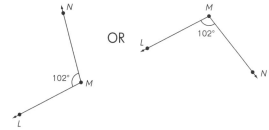

OR

9.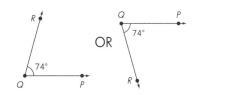

OR

10.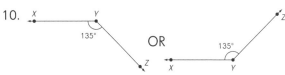

OR

Lesson 9.3

1. $\frac{1}{4}$-turn

2. $\frac{1}{2}$-turn

3. $\frac{3}{4}$-turn

4. 360°

5. 270°

6. 90°

7. 180°

8. Thinking Skill − Spatial visualization
    south → west → north
    Samantha ends up facing north.

9. Thinking Skill − Spatial visualization
    west → south → north
    Dino ends up facing north.

Put on Your Thinking Cap!

1. 65°

2. 51°

3. 23°

4. There are 14 squares or rectangles.
   14 × 4 = 56 right angles

5. Thinking skills: Comparing

Figures	Number of Angles Smaller than a Right Angle	Number of Angles Larger than a Right Angle
a.	2	1
b.	5	2
c.	9	3
d.	13	5

Chapter 10

Lesson 10.1

1.

2.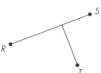

3.

4.

5. 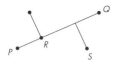   OR

6. A triangle OR a right triangle

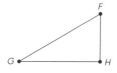

Lesson 10.2

1.

2.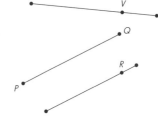

3.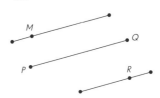

4. Yes

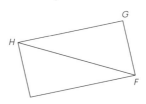

5. A rectangle

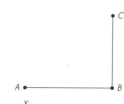

Lesson 10.3

1. Horizontal line segments: $\overline{SR}$; $\overline{PQ}$; $\overline{MK}$
2. Vertical line segments: $\overline{SP}$; $\overline{RQ}$; $\overline{MN}$
3. Horizontal line segments: $\overline{AB}$; $\overline{FE}$
   Vertical line segments: $\overline{AF}$; $\overline{BC}$
4. Horizontal line segments: $\overline{LM}$; $\overline{ON}$
   Vertical line segments: $\overline{LK}$; $\overline{MN}$
5. Horizontal line segments: $\overline{QR}$; $\overline{PV}$
   Vertical line segments: $\overline{UV}$; $\overline{RS}$

6.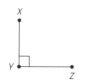

7.

8. A vertical line segment is always perpendicular to a horizontal line segment if they are both drawn on the same sheet of paper.

Put on Your Thinking Cap!

1. Perpendicular line segments: $\overline{AB}$ and $\overline{EF}$; $\overline{AJ}$ and $\overline{EF}$; $\overline{AB}$ and $\overline{GH}$; $\overline{AJ}$ and $\overline{GH}$; $\overline{CD}$ and $\overline{EF}$; $\overline{CD}$ and $\overline{GH}$

2. Parallel line segments: $\overline{AB}$ and $\overline{CD}$; $\overline{EF}$ and $\overline{GH}$; $\overline{KL}$ and $\overline{YZ}$; $\overline{IJ}$ and $\overline{ML}$

3. 12th Street

4. 8th Street, Houston Street, and 5th Avenue

5. 15th Avenue, 8th Street, 5th Avenue, and Houston Street

6. 20 right angles

7. 32 right angles
Pattern: Add 6 matchsticks each time.
OR Each figure has 6 more matchsticks.

8.

Figure	1	2	3	4	5	6	7	8	9	10
No. of Right Angles	2	8	14	20	26	32	38	44	50	56

9. $2 + 6 \times (20 - 1)$
$= 2 + 6 \times 19$
$= 116$ right angles

10. $2 + 6 \times (n - 1)$ right angles
OR $(6n - 4)$ right angles

Chapter 11

Lesson 11.1

1. 4
2. 4
3. 2
4. square
5. 4
6. equal OR parallel
7. 2
8. rectangle
9. 0
10. equal OR parallel

11. 2
12. No. There are four right angles in a rectangle.
13. 0
14. 4
15. 2
16. No. There are four right angles in a square.
17. 0
18. 1
19. No. There are four right angles in a rectangle.
20. 6
21. 3
22. 6
23. 6
24. 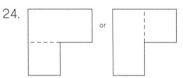 or
25.
26.
27.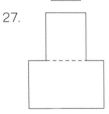
28.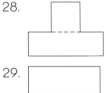
29.
30.

31.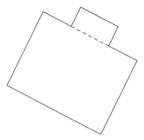

32.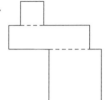

33.

34.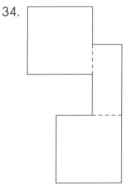

Lesson 11.2

1. 52°
2. 26°
3. 58°
4. 45°
5. HG = 11 cm; DE = 4 cm
6. ST = 16 cm; RS = 14 cm
7. AJ = 19 cm; HG = 17 cm

Put on Your Thinking Cap!

1. There are fifteen 1 × 1 squares, eight 2 × 2 squares, and three 3 × 3 squares.
   15 + 8 + 3 = 26 squares
2. 11
3. 5 cm

4.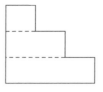

Test Prep for Chapters 7 to 11

Multiple Choice

1. A
2. B
3. D
4. B
5. D
6. D
7. C
8. B
9. D
10. B

Short Answer

11. $\overline{HG}//\overline{NM}$; $\overline{CD} \perp \overline{HG}$ or $\overline{CD} \perp \overline{NM}$
12. 55
13. 26
14. 0.06
15. $5\frac{3}{4}$
16. 14.03
17. 3.6
18. 3.8
19. 134.6 centimeters
20. $10.60

Extended Response

21.
$$\boxed{} \xrightarrow{\div 8} \boxed{} \xrightarrow{-34.7} \boxed{45.3}$$

$45.3 + 34.7 = 80$

$80 \times 8 = 640$

The number is 640.

22. $1.88 \text{ m} + 2.45 \text{ m} = 4.33 \text{ meters}$

$10.00 \text{ m} - 4.33 \text{ m} = 5.67 \text{ meters}$

Nicole has 5.67 meters of ribbon left.

23. $14.2 - 8.3 = 5.9 \text{ kilograms}$

$10.7 - 5.9 = 4.8 \text{ kilograms}$

The mass of Parcel B is 4.8 kilograms.

Chapter 12

Lesson 12.1

1. $2; 5; 2 \times 5 = 10; 10; 10$

2. $1; 7; 1 \times 7 = 7; 7; 7$

3. $6; 3; 6 \times 3 = 18; 18; 18$

4. $4 \times 4; 16; 16$

5. $12 \times 6; 72; 72$

6. $18; 20$

7. $34; 70$

8. $32; 64$

9. $30; 54$

10. Area $= 20 \times 8 = 160 \text{ m}^2$

11. Area $= 10 \times 4 = 40 \text{ m}^2$

12. Area of wrapping paper $= 60 \times 9$
$= 540 \text{ cm}^2$

Area of wrapping paper used for gift $= 540 \div 2$
$= 270 \text{ cm}^2$

Area of leftover paper $= 540 - 270$
$= 270 \text{ cm}^2$

13. Length of each square table $= 12 \div 4 = 3 \text{ ft}$
Area of each square table $= 3 \times 3 = 9 \text{ ft}^2$

14. Perimeter of garden $= 15 \times 2 + 22 \times 2$
$= 30 + 44 = 74 \text{ m}$

Cost of putting up a fence $= 74 \times \$10$
$= \$740$

15. 5 to 6 unit^2

16. 7 to 8 unit^2

17. 9 to 10 unit^2

18. 7 to 8 unit^2

19. 14 to 15 unit^2

20. 12 to 13 unit^2

Lesson 12.2 (Part 1)

1. $8 + 4 + 8 + 4 = 24 \text{ cm}; 24$

2. $4 \times 7 = 28 \text{ in.}; 28$

3. $64 \div 4 = 16 \text{ in.}$

4. $40 \div 4 = 10 \text{ cm}$

5. $100 \div 2 = 50 \text{ cm}$
$50 - 18 = 32 \text{ cm}$

6. $108 \div 2 = 54 \text{ cm}$
$54 - 36 = 18 \text{ cm}$

Lesson 12.2 (Part 2)

1. $13 \times 5 = 65 \text{ ft}^2; 65$

2. $3 \times 3 = 9 \text{ cm}^2; 9$

3. $126 \div 9 = 14 \text{ yd}$

4. $9 \times 9 = 81 \text{ m}^2$
Length of one side of the square is 9 meters.

5. a. $12 \times 12 = 144 \text{ cm}^2$
Length of each side of the poster is
12 centimeters.
b. Perimeter $= 12 \times 4 = 48 \text{ cm}$

6. a. Width $= 200 \div 20 = 10 \text{ cm}$
b. Perimeter $= 20 \times 2 + 10 \times 2$
$= 40 + 20 = 60 \text{ cm}$

7. a. Length $= 240 \div 15 = 16 \text{ yd}$
b. Perimeter $= 16 \times 2 + 15 \times 2$
$= 32 + 30$
$= 62 \text{ yd}$

8. a. $11 \times 11 = 121 \text{ m}^2$
Length of each side of the pond is 11 meters.
b. Perimeter $= 11 \times 4 = 44 \text{ m}$

9. a. $52 \div 2 = 26 \text{ cm}$
Length $= 26 - 10 = 16 \text{ cm}$
b. Area $= 16 \times 10 = 160 \text{ cm}^2$

10. a. $54 \div 2 = 27 \text{ in.}$
Length $= 2 \text{ units}$
Width $= 1 \text{ unit}$
3 units $= 27 \text{ in.}$
1 unit $= 27 \div 3 = 9 \text{ in.}$ (Width)
2 units $= 9 \times 2 = 18 \text{ in.}$ (Length)
b. Area $= 18 \times 9 = 162 \text{ in.}^2$

Lesson 12.3

1. $4; 6; 14; 58$

2. $7; 8; 20; 70$

3. 54

4. 28

5. Area = $8 \times 8 + 8 \times 3 = 64 + 24 = 88$ in.^{2}

6. Area = $4 \times 3 + 6 \times 8 = 12 + 48 = 60$ yd^2

7. Area = $10 \times 6 + 3 \times 7 = 60 + 21 = 81$ ft^2

8. Area = $1 \times 1 + 6 \times 3 + 3 \times 2$
   $= 1 + 18 + 6 = 25$ m^2

Lesson 12.4

1. a. 15 m^2 to 17 m^2
   b. $3 \times 5 = 15$ m^2 (insufficient)
   $3 \times 6 = 18$ m^2
   Length of wallpaper needed is 6 meters.

2. a. 8 m^2 to 10 m^2
   b. $8 \times \$10 = \$80$

3. $12 \times 7 = 84$ in.^{2}
   $84 + 87 = 171$ in.^{2}
   171 in.^{2}

4. $28 \times 28 = 784$ ft^2
   $16 \times 16 = 256$ ft^2
   $784 - 256 = 528$ ft^2
   528 ft^2

5. Area of whole figure = $8 \times 7 + 8 \times 14$
   $= 56 + 112 = 168$ m^2
   Area of unshaded figure = $168 - 39$
   $= 129$ m^2

6. Area of large rectangle = 17×10
   $= 170$ yd^2
   Area of small rectangle = 15×8
   $= 120$ yd^2
   Area of path = $170 - 120 = 50$ yd^2

7. a. Area of each square = $405 \div 5$
   $= 81$ in.^{2}
   b. Length of each square is 9 inches.
   Perimeter of figure = $9 \times 12 = 108$ in.

8. a. Area of table = $2 \times 1 = 2$ m^2
   b. Perimeter of room = $4 \times 2 + 3 \times 2$
   $= 8 + 6 = 14$ m

Put on Your Thinking Cap!

1. $384 \div 8 = 48$ in.
   $\frac{1}{4} \times 48 = 12$ cm
   a. $12 \times 8 = 96$ in.^{2}
   b. $8 + 12 + 48 + 8 + 12 + 48 = 136$ in.

2. Strategy: Draw a diagram.
   Solution: The length of the 4 small squares
   $= 4 \times 4 = 16$ in.
   The length of the shaded square
   $= 16 - 9 = 7$ in.
   The area of the shaded square $= 7 \times 7$
   $= 49$ in^2.
   The shaded area is 49 square inches.

3. Strategy: Guess and check
   Solution: $288 \div 9 = 32$ cm^2
   Area of each rectangle is 32 cm^2.
   Guess and check to find the width and length
   of each of the 9 identical rectangles. First,
   observe that the length of each rectangle is twice
   its width.
   $32 = 1 \times 32$ (32 is not twice of 1)
   $= 2 \times 16$ (16 is not twice of 2)
   $= 4 \times 8$ (8 is twice of 4)
   So, the width and length can only be
   4 centimeters and 8 centimeters, respectively.
   Width of the figure: $8 + 4 = 12$ cm
   Length of the figure: $4 \times 6 = 24$ cm
   Perimeter of the figure = $24 + 12 + 24 + 12$
   $= 72$ cm

Chapter 13

Lesson 13.1

1. Yes

2. Yes

3. No

4. Yes

5. No

6. No

7. Yes

8. Yes

9. Yes

10. No

11. No

12. No

Lesson 13.2

1. Yes
2. No
3. Yes
4. No
5. Yes
6. Yes
7. Yes
8. No
9. Yes
10. Yes
11. No
12. No
13. No
14. No

Lesson 13.3

1.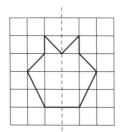

2.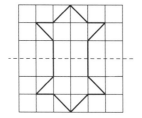

3.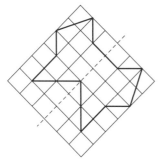

4.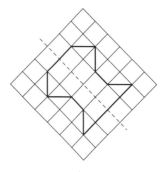

5.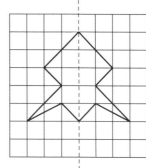

6.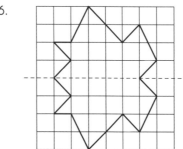

7.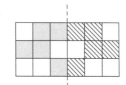

8.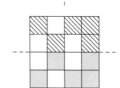

9.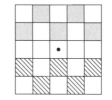

10.

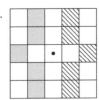

Put on Your Thinking Cap!

1.

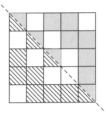

2.

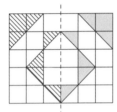

3. Accept any possible answer.

4.

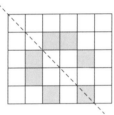

5. Answers vary. Sample:

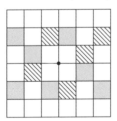

6. Answers vary. Sample:

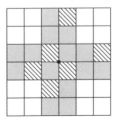

Chapter 14

Lesson 14.1

1.

2.

3.

4. Yes. It is made up of a single repeated shape. The repeated shapes do not have gaps between them nor do they overlap.

5. No. There are gaps between the repeated shapes.

6. No. the repeated shapes overlap.

7.

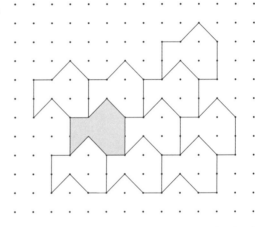

8.

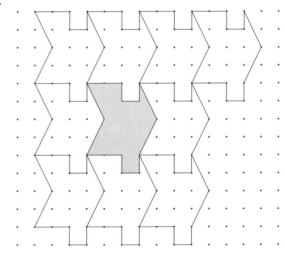

9.

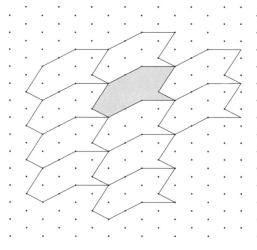

12.

10.

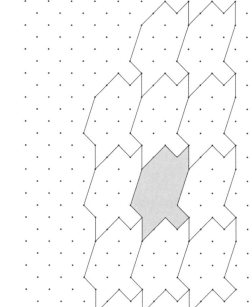

13. Answers vary. Sample:

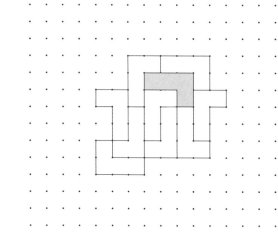

11.

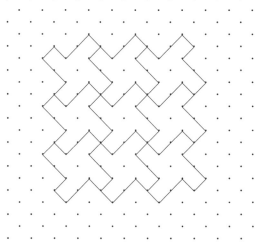

14.

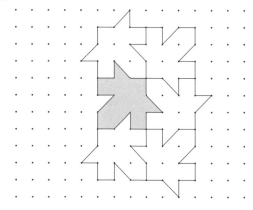

Lesson 14.2

1.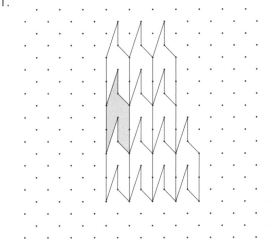

2.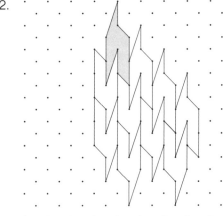

3.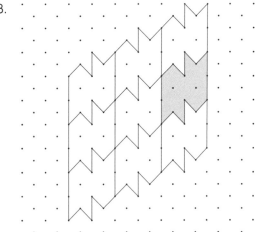

4.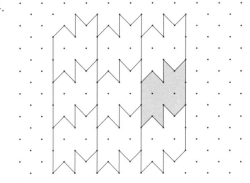

5.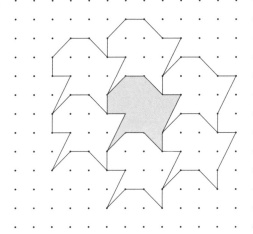

Put on Your Thinking Cap!

1. Accept any correct tessellation.

2. Thinking Skill: Transformation

   Strategy: Repeated patterns

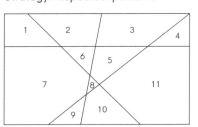

3. Thinking Skill: Identifying patterns and
              relationships
    Strategy: Look for a pattern

Number of lines	Maximum number of sections obtained	Pattern observed	
1	2	$1 + 1 = 2$	$1 + \dfrac{1 \times 2}{2} = 2$
2	4	$1 + 1 + 2 = 4$	$1 + \dfrac{2 \times 3}{2} = 4$
3	7	$1 + 1 + 2 + 3 = 7$	$1 + \dfrac{3 \times 4}{2} = 7$
4	11	$1 + 1 + 2 + 3 + 4 = 11$	$1 + \dfrac{4 \times 5}{2} = 11$
5	16	$1 + 1 + 2 + 3 + 4 + 5 = 16$	$1 + \dfrac{5 \times 6}{2} = 16$
6	22	$1 + 1 + 2 + 3 + 4 + 5 + 6 = 22$	$1 + \dfrac{6 \times 7}{2} = 22$

End-of-Year Test

Multiple Choice

1. C	2. A
3. C	4. B
5. C	6. A
7. D	8. C
9. C	10. C
11. A	12. D
13. C	14. C
15. D	16. B
17. A	18. D
19. C	20. D

Short Answer

21. 21.60, 21.06, 20.60, 20.06
22. a. 26
    b. 27
23. $\dfrac{1}{3}$
24.

25.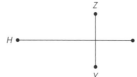

26. 16.8
27.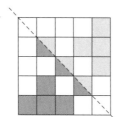

28. 6.38
29. 45
30. 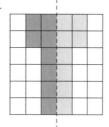   31.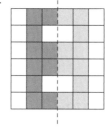

32.

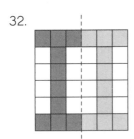

33. $90 \div 6 = 15$
    $64 \div 6 \approx 10$
    $15 \times 10 = 150$ squares

34. 3

35. 48

36. 44°

37. Jason

38. 14

39. 13

40.

Extended Response

41.

Ann

Brian   56   } 544 beads

Cindy   34

$544 - 34 - 34 - 56 = 420$
$420 \div 3 = 140$ beads (Cindy)
$140 + 34 + 56 = 230$ beads (Ann)
Ann has 230 beads.

42. $24 \div 4 = 6$ centimeters
    $42 - 6 \times 2 = 30$ centimeters
    $30 \div 2 = 15$ centimeters
    Length of the rectangle is 15 centimeters.

43. $16 \times 4 = 64$ ft
    $64 - 19 \times 2 = 26$ ft
    $26 \div 2 = 13$ ft
    $19 \times 13 = 247$ ft^2
    Area of the rectangle is 247 ft^2.

44. $25 \times 20 = 500$ m^2; $23 \times 18 = 414$ m^2
    a. 500 m^2 $- 414$ m^2 $= 86$ m^2
    b. $86 \times \$27 = \$2,322$

45. Make a list of multiplies of 4:
    4, 8, 12, 16, 20, 24, 28, 32, 36
    $20 + 32 = 52$
    Side length of smaller square
    $= 20$ cm $\div 4 = 5$ cm
    Side length of larger square
    $= 32$ cm $\div 4 = 8$ cm
    5 cm $\times 5$ cm $= 25$ cm^2
    8 cm $\times 8$ cm $= 64$ cm^2
    64 cm^2 $- 25$ cm^2 $= 39$ cm^2
    The area of the shaded part is 39 cm^2.

    OR
    $24 + 28 = 52$
    Side length of smaller square
    $= 24$ cm $\div 4 = 6$ cm
    Side length of larger square
    $= 28$ cm $\div 4 = 7$ cm
    6 cm $\times 6$ cm $= 36$ cm^2
    7 cm $\times 7$ cm $= 49$ cm^2
    49 cm^2 $- 36$ cm^2 $= 13$ cm^2
    The area of the shaded part is 13 cm^2.

    OR
    $16 + 36 = 52$
    Side length of smaller square
    $= 16$ cm $\div 4 = 4$ cm
    Side length of larger square
    $= 36$ cm $\div 4 = 9$ cm
    4 cm $\times 4$ cm $= 16$ cm^2
    9 cm $\times 9$ cm $= 81$ cm^2
    81 cm^2 $- 16$ cm^2 $= 65$ cm^2
    The area of the shaded part is 65 cm^2.